I find Alan's writing positive and in tune with our needs today. I trust he will continue in his good work as I do mine. Together, we're bound to make a difference!

**Leo Buscaglia**, author of *Living, Loving, and Learning*

I loved *The Dragon!* Thanks for a great contribution. I want powerful, enlightened, conscious people to read and *apply* our messages.

**Dr. Wayne W. Dyer**, author of *Your Erroneous Zones*

The way Alan Cohen shares his heart in his books and tapes is a positive and dynamic force which is making significant contributions to healing humanity. It is important that his books be read by many people!

**Dr. Jerry Jampolsky**, author of *Love is Letting Go of Fear*

Alan Cohen has a rare and precious quality: He inspires happiness, and his message is as pure as his heart.

**Hugh Prather**, author of *Notes to Myself*

Alan Cohen is one of the most gentle and powerful guiding lights of the profound transition now occurring on earth. His writing will give you the courage to release all fear and allow yourself to be lifted naturally to the next stage of human evolution.

**Barbara Marx Hubbard**, visionary and peace activist

I think Alan's work is very insightful and helpful. Many people have told me how they have grown as a result of his books and tapes. Alan's teaching has brought peace and fulfillment to thousands, and I heartily endorse it!

**Wally "Famous" Amos**, cookie magnate and
motivational teacher

# BY ALAN COHEN

## *Books:*

Are You As Happy As Your Dog?
Companions of the Heart
Dare to Be Yourself
*A Deep Breath of Life
The Dragon Doesn't Live Here Anymore
Have You Hugged Your Monster Today?
I Had It All the Time
*Joy Is My Compass
*Lifestyles of the Rich in Spirit
The Peace That You Seek
*Rising in Love
Setting the Seen

## *Audiocassettes:*

Deep Relaxation
*The Dragon Doesn't Live Here Anymore (audio book)
Eden Morning
I Believe in You
*I Had It All the Time (audio book)
Journey to the Center of the Heart (also available as a CD)
Peace

## *Videocassette:*

*Dare to Be Yourself*

(All of the above are available through Alan Cohen Publications: 800-462-3013. Items marked with an asterisk may also be ordered by calling Hay House at 800-654-5126.)

# JOY IS MY
# COMPASS

Published and distributed in the United States by: Hay House, Inc.,
P.O. Box 5100, Carlsbad, CA 92018-5100
(800) 654-5126 • (800) 650-5115 (fax)

Cover illustration: Barbara Lambase          Cover design: Christy Allison

The author wishes to acknowledge the contributors listed below for their kind
permission to reprint their copyrighted material. All materials used by permission. All rights reserved.

Illustration on page 10, ©1987, Erkki Alanen; Angelight Music, lyrics from
"Take Your Power Back," by Charley Thweatt, ©1988, Angelight Music; The
Crossroad Publishing Company, excerpt from *Tales of a Magic Monastery,* by
Brother Theophane, ©1981 Cistercian Abbey of Spencer, Inc.; Golden Quest,
photos of Hilda Charlton; Inner Harmony Music, permission to adapt from lyrics
of "Joy Is My Compass," ©1989 Michael Stillwater.

**Library of Congress Cataloging-in-Publication Data**

Cohen, Alan, 1950-
     Joy is my compass   :   taking the risk to follow your bliss   /
Alan Cohen.
        p.     cm.
     ISBN 1-56170-341-9  (trade paper)
     1. Meditations.   I.  Title.
BL624.2.C644    1996
291.4'3—dc20                        96-38824
                                          CIP

ISBN 1-56170-341-9

00 99 98 97 96    5 4 3 2 1
First Printing, 1990, by Alan Cohen Publications
First Printing, Revised Edition, November 1996, Hay House, Inc.

# JOY IS MY COMPASS

## TAKING THE RISK TO FOLLOW YOUR BLISS

# ALAN COHEN

Hay House, Inc.
Carlsbad, CA

# Foreword by Joyce and Barry Vissell

In the Spring of 1985, our Unity minister asked us if we would do a favor for her. A guest speaker was coming in two weeks, and he needed a place to stay overnight. She wondered aloud, "I just don't know what I shall do with Alan Cohen."

When we heard the name, a bolt of energy went through both of us. Suddenly we felt very joyous. "He can stay with us," we offered. Neither of us had ever heard of Alan Cohen before, yet the feeling that came with his name was warm and comfortable to us.

Driving home, we began to talk about our expected visitor, and wondered what he was like. Instantly we felt, without any doubt, that we were about to enter into a close relationship with our "unknown" friend. We had never felt so attracted to a person's joy and light, all the while not knowing anything about him.

Upon arriving home we told our two children, Rami and Mira, about our guest. The girls felt excited, too. Rami jumped up and said, "Oh, I just know I'm going to love this man." Mira asked, "Is he like Santa Claus?"

In the days that followed, a happy anticipation of meeting Alan Cohen grew. Finally the big day arrived! We met Alan at his lecture, and instantly we felt reunited with a dear kindred spirit. (To Mira's disappointment, he did not look like Santa Claus. However, his jolly manner had us laughing most of the night.) After the lecture we sat together in our home and affirmed the depth and importance of our connection.

Since that time, we have read all of Alan's books and delighted in each one. Sometimes we enjoy reading passages to one another before going to sleep. We have attended Alan's lectures and retreats, and we have grown from them, as well. Truly this gentle man sees Spirit through the eyes of love, as we do.

The fondest times, however, are the times we have had alone with Alan. Along with our playful times, we have seen him face challenges like any human being. What impresses us most about Alan is that even in difficult times, there is a beautiful light about him. His thoughts are still with God and he returns to the strength of that connection. Over and over, he has demonstrated to us that joy is his compass.

We are inspired by Alan's willingness to confront and transform pain when it comes along, rather than run from it. This requires a great deal of courage. Many of us want our life's path to be one of joy and lightness only. We don't realize that earth is also a schoolroom where we have to learn all the lessons. When we are willing to look at, embrace, and learn from the challenging feelings in our lives— sadness, grief, fear—then we find that our capacity for joy and love is actually increased.

In this important book, Alan Cohen transforms everyday life situations into opportunities for growth and healing. In his clear, intimate, and humorous style, Alan demonstrates how to live from the heart. He shows us all how to make joy a dancing partner in our lives.

Joyce Vissell, RN, MS
Barry Vissell, MD
authors of *The Shared Heart,*
*Models of Love,* and
*Risk to be Healed*

# Introduction

One of the questions I am most frequently asked is: "When I have to make an important decision, how can I know which inner voice is the correct one?"

Many of us have grown up with a host of "shoulds," "oughts," and a long list of suppositions about "what a good person would do in this situation." But the real question is not what your parents, friends, teachers, or minister would do; the real question is: "What would you like to do?" Although this question is the most important one in any decision-making process, it is often the last asked and the least considered.

This book poses a bold assertion: Within you rests all the guidance you need to carry you through life with a sense of purpose, aliveness, and celebration. While books, teachers, and classes may assist you, ultimately you must turn within for the guidance to fulfill the personal destiny you choose. Our heart speaks to us most clearly not through admonitions or punishment, but through the voice of sheer joy. Can you believe that the way to be in your right place in life is to do what makes you happy?

If you are ready to dump guilt, fear, and pain, read on. The stories between these covers illuminate people who have chosen aliveness as their motivator, and approach their daily activities and relationships with a sense of delight and adventure. These people have learned how to go beyond hardship and challenge and follow the light home. These people have learned how to live.

While in recent years the media has paid considerable attention to Near-Death Experiences, this book probes an even more exciting phenomena: Near-Life Experiences. Rumor has it that there are a number of people on the planet who have come very close to living—and are still here to tell about it. You will read about them here, and if you follow their example, you may become one of them!

If you are at an important crossroads in your life, you are being challenged to make the all-important choice between what others want or expect you to be, and who you are. One signpost is marked "fear" and the other "joy." Love yourself enough to make yourself happy, and you will always be grateful you followed your path with heart.

— *Alan Cohen*

# Acknowledgements

It seems natural that a book devoted to joy should unfold in the most joyous way possible. I have been blessed to share this production with people whose hearts and minds have been open, joyful, and intent on creating a work that would heal and uplift all who read it. I offer my heartfelt thanks to the following friends and associates who have assisted me in following my joy compass:

Karren Houser, for her boundless enthusiasm and sparkling support of me as a person, writer, and healer; and for being a teacher of joy and delight.

Sara Patton, whose editorial assistance has been a precious wing that has made this project fly.

Paulette de Maestre, whose managerial expertise has brought these ideas to the reader in the most purposeful way.

Judy Ivec and Joan Fericy, whose office assistance has been a blessing through their delightful spirit as well as their skills.

Valerie Johnson, for her angelic and accurate typesetting service.

The publishers of *New Frontier, Unity, New Realities, Visions, Holistic Living,* and *The American Holistic Medical Association* newsletter for their invitations to share my ideas.

Barry and Joyce Vissell, for their loving friendship and kind foreword.

Joyce Weibel, for her magnificent cover photograph.

Rev. Robert Hudson, who originally introduced me to the concept, "joy is my compass."

Carla Gordan and Mary, for their generous friendship, mediumship, and spiritual support.

Rosie and Garren, Shanera, Noah, Munchie, Yogi, the dolphins and whales, and the other free-spirited creatures who play in the Kingdom.

Maloah and Michael Stillwater, Charley and Lori Thweatt, Stephen Longfellow Fiske, and the other co-teachers with whom I share workshops and retreats.

Haven Boggs, Patch Adams, Terry Cole-Whittaker, Scott Kalechstein, Swami Beyondananda, and all the people who have been wise enough to be silly and demonstrate that having fun is more important than looking good.

You, the reader, for allowing me to fulfill my function as a teacher of love.

*To Mary,*
*who has shown me the light of my soul*
*by reminding me that*
*playing is as important as praying*

*Joy is my compass*
*I'm taking the risk to follow my bliss*
*I'm making a start to follow my heart*
*And I'm ready now*

*Joy is my compass*
*It leads me everywhere I need to go*
*It shows me everything I need to know*
*It's my highway home to the Kingdom*

*Joy is my compass*
*My spirit is singing!*
*My heartsong is ringing!*
*The song of my soul is bringing me home.*

by Michael Stillwater and Alan Cohen

# Section One

# *Joy Is My Compass*

# JOY IS
# MY COMPASS

*The road to healing begins not with a*
*blind leap outward, but a gentle step inward.*

*The Guru*

I have a new guru. Her name is Shanera, which is the name of an angel. She has big brown saucer eyes, a perfect turned-up nose, and long sandy hair. The guru is five years old. She is one of the wisest teachers I have ever had, and by far the simplest.

Shanera and I met when her mom visited my home at a time when I was needing a friend. From the moment I met this guru I was impressed by her unwillingness to be fooled by the seriousness of the world. When she entered my home she was not the least bit interested in routine conversations on age, weather, or what she did in school today. Instead, she went right for the Olie Muppet Puppet peeking out in the corner below the kitchen counter.

Shanera and I have become the best of buddies, travelling companions of a sort. I don't feel that I have much to teach her in the way of information, but my delight in being with her is a gift to both of us. It is a very natural relationship.

One night Shanera and I were sitting on the couch, and I was reading her a bedtime story.

"What are you going to do when you get up tomorrow morning?" the guru asked.

Hmmm. "As soon as I get up, I will meditate."

"Oh," she responded. "Then what?"

"Then I'll probably take a shower."

"Then what?"

"Then I usually do my yoga."

"Then what?"

The child was persistent. OK, I'm game. "Then it's time for breakfast."

Her saucer eyes were twinkling. "Then what will you do?"

"Then I think I'll go to the beach."

Before she asked again, I figured I would turn the tables on her and see what her plans were. "How about you? What are *you* going to do tomorrow?"

"I'm gonna play! That's all I do is play! I play from the moment I get up in the morning till the moment I go to sleep at night! What a silly question!"

I was nailed. Nailed to a cross of therapeutic techniques. Here were all of my plans to lighten up, to get free, to learn to be happy—all my methods to work my way toward more fun in my life. But the guru needed no preparation and no method. Her method was the goal itself—play. She is a human *being*, not a human *preparing*. She clearly honors herself and the light that shines through her. She knows she deserves to be happy now. Perhaps that is why "guru" is spelled G...U...R...U... *Gee, you are you!*

I learned the same lesson from a friend of mine who is a Unity minister. I asked him, "Bob, how do you make your important decisions? When you are feeling unsure which direction to take, what do you use for a guide?"

Bob immediately lit up and answered, "Joy is my compass." He smiled an impishly angelic smile and explained, "Whenever I have a choice to make, I ask myself, 'Which alternative makes me feel the most joyful?' Then I try each of the choices on for size. Usually there is one that feels lighter, freer, more like the real me. It feels like coming home. Then I know that is the direction that God wants me to go."

I was fascinated. It was an amazingly simple yet powerful way to choose. I was struck by the innocence of Spirit's way.

Bob continued, "Then I step out on faith, knowing that God would rather teach me by happiness than by suffering. I have been following the joy voice for a long time now, and I have never been sorry. I know that God leads me through life to my highest good by lighting up the path of my best interests with joy."

What a marvelous way to live! I loved the idea—it cut quickly through the intellect and proceeded directly to the heart. Since that day I have adopted joy as my compass, too. And I have found that it does indeed work. Following the joy has been the most direct way to fulfilling my life's purpose. It is the affirmation that God wants me to be alive, and that His voice is ever-willing to direct me to more and greater life.

There is no predicting where the joy compass will point, or what form the happiness is to come through. Sometimes the compass directs me to go out dancing, or take a leisurely tube ride down a river, or go see a Steve Martin movie on a moment's flash of enthusiasm. Sometimes the voice of joy calls me to simply be still and take time to listen to the river that flows behind my thoughts. And sometimes joy attracts me to clean the bathtub, go jogging, or call a friend with whom I need to heal a relationship. I am continually amazed at how Spirit brings me peace through doing the things that need to be done.

Perhaps next to our calendar, computer, or mirror, we should keep a joy compass. We have so many outer guides, gurus, and reminders of what we need to do. There are tons of books, hordes of psychic consultants to read our orbs and auras, and an endless array of methods and trainings to assist us in finding our way to our highest good. But not one of them is as accurate, available, or valuable as the voice for love that resides within our very heart. Even the best of gurus can do no more than remind us of what we already know.

It is time for us to remember how powerful we really are and start living our lives more fully. Many of us have been students long enough. We are ready to put what we've learned into action. The road to healing begins not with a blind leap outward, but a gentle step inward. Nothing in the outer world can match the quality or integrity of what you and I already know. The outer world is but a mirror for the inner life. Our search for answers begins and ends with none other than our own self, and the most direct way to discover that self is to follow the path of joy.

# WHAT THEY
# SERVE IN HEAVEN

*Something happened to me when I
let it all be OK. I felt relief. My heart
opened. I was at peace. I had found the
answer to all of life: Just let it be.*

Every great master has had his moment of enlightenment. Moses found God within the burning bush. Buddha saw the truth after fasting under the Bodhi tree. Jesus, we are told, became the Christ when the dove of Spirit descended upon him at the moment of his baptism.

I found my revelation at McDonald's. Strange though it may sound, I had my date with destiny under those arches of gold. No McKidding.

One breezy Saturday afternoon I found myself touched by the angel of hunger while driving south on the Garden State Parkway. Realizing that there was no choice other than McDonald's, I flicked my blinker in the direction of hamburger heaven and steered straight for the beef.

I strode in for my fast-food fix. To my dismay, I discovered that it was Family Day, which brought with it a platoon of children practicing a host of fascinating methods to gain their parents' attention. Amid this prepubescent circus there was even a birthday party taking place. I mean, there were *lots* of kids!

I instantly felt stifled and righteously irritated. "Where did all these kids come from?" I pondered, seeking a little corner of the restaurant where I could eat in peace.

As I began salting my French fries, I remembered that someone had told me that McDonald's puts sugar in their fries. "Gross!" I thought. "Why do they have to put sugar in everything?" I complained to the Spirit of Adelle Davis. My irritation grew.

Then I glanced at the four-color cardboard containing my hot apple pie. I found no listing of ingredients, and concluded that there were probably so many chemicals and preservatives that McDonald's neatly omitted naming any of them. "Hrrmmph," I muttered, "—more deception!"

Then I saw something I had never noticed before. I was sitting near a life-sized plastic statue of Ronald McDonald. The shiny character was repeating a tape loop of ridiculous jokes to a bunch of squally kids surrounding him in a caged area. Not only that, but Ronald's designers had programmed a crazy laugh to follow each of the cornball offerings. The whole scene felt like a cross between *Amazing Stories* and *The Twilight Zone*.

"This takes the cake," I thought. "I'm never coming here again—bad vibes!"

Then something happened—something very precious, something holy, something that changed my life. Sitting there in the smog of my

11

own thoughts, a little voice within my soul spoke to me. It asked but one question, and it was the one that made all the difference.

*"What if this were all OK?"* the gentle voice whispered.

"What do you mean, *'all OK?'* " my conscious mind retorted. "This scene is weird."

*"Think again,"* that noble voice gently urged. *"Imagine—just imagine for a moment—that all of this is OK, and that none of what you see around you holds any real threat to who you are or your power to be happy now. Imagine that your safety remains quite inviolate even in the midst of this story line."*

Now, that was interesting. I did feel a breeze of peace as I considered this notion.

I began to reconsider the scene, attempting to look at it in this new and different light. I pondered the thought that sugar has no real power to affect my ability to love. I considered that the list of loving attributes of the God within me is longer than the list of preservatives in the pie. And how would I feel if I knew there was no real harm in that plastic toy telling silly jokes to those kids?

I shifted my attention to the kids playing with Ronald McDonald. They were laughing. They were happy. They were in heaven. I enjoyed watching them.

Something happened to me when I let it all be OK. I felt relief. My heart opened. I was at peace. I had found the answer to being there. I had found the answer to all of life: Just let it be.

I got in line for some more French fries and apple pie. That's what they serve in heaven, I found out.

# A DREAM
# COME TRUE

*Some of the most powerful prayers are
happiness, joy, song, and laughter.
Whenever someone loves, God
is present on earth.*

At a workshop I was presenting in a Florida church, someone handed me a note during intermission. Written on the back of an envelope, the message declared, *"Song, joy, and laughter in church—a dream come true!"*

The poignant simplicity of the message rang through me. It occurred to me that song, joy, and laughter have been conspicuously absent from a lot of the churches we have attended. Many of us believed that song was standing and reading ancient words from a hymnal, joy was smiling politely at the minister as we departed, and laughter was definitely something you don't do in church.

What *did* we do in church?

I know two girls who were forced to bow at the altar for so long that they gnawed their initials into the altar steps with their teeth. Others used Sunday school as a practice field for torturing smaller children with pick-up-sticks. The big thrill for the boys in our Hebrew school was sneaking up on tween-age girls and snapping the backs of their training bras.

Perhaps the ultimate statement of commando communion tactics was depicted in *The Blues Brothers*. In that classic film about two hardened criminals, the only thing that strikes terror in the hearts of Jake and Elwood Blues is the prospect of going back to visit their Catholic school principal—*the Penguin*, as they call her.

Trembling, the scofflaws enter the Penguin's office with their knuckles well-protected behind their backs. But alas, to no avail. When Jake (John Belushi) says a bad word, out comes the ruler, and the jig is up for the Blues Brothers. Like an evangelistic Errol Flynn, the Penguin swashbuckles the heathens into submission, and sends them rolling down the stairs and out the door into the wilds of Chicago. No wonder they're called the Blues Brothers.

What to do with old feelings of pain and hurt about religion? Perhaps we can, as Michael Stillwater sings, turn our "Blues into Gold."[1] We can take an old, seemingly limiting form, and look at it again to find a blessing. We can look at our history, learn from it, and create a new destiny.

One of the gifts of a painful experience is to translate it into a valuable lesson. There is a way to live without pain. God is a God of joy; laughter glorifies God in a most noble way. Worshipping a God of happiness, rather than punishment, makes the church a place of sanctuary—a haven from fear, not an altar to it. A real house of God is a place where we can feel relaxed, knowing that we are free of the judgments that we have learned to place on ourselves. Songs and laughter glorify God as a teacher of release, not bondage. As Saint Ignatius taught, "The glory of God is humankind fully alive." Church is not a place to learn about *going* to heaven: It is a place where we can *be* in heaven.

I wonder if Jesus ever meant to start an organization. He walked in dignity, without dogma. He carried the church with him wherever he went. Wherever the master spoke, the church was there. When Jesus referred to "my church," he meant all the people who loved him, who were touched by his teaching, and who wanted to live the life he exemplified. He was a man whose humility spoke far louder than the pomp to which those around him had become subservient. He took comfort not in the respect that others showed him, but in the worthiness that he found within himself as a Son of God. He had one goal: to love everyone he met so purely that they would catch his vision of their perfection.

To be a member of a church or temple of any kind is a very holy opportunity. Ideally, church is an organization that is totally dedicated to the awareness and glorification of God. It is designed to bring heaven to earth. This is a lofty goal indeed, and must be approached with an attitude of reverence and celebration.

Matthew Fox, a Catholic priest, has made a powerful stand for what he calls "creation-centered spirituality."[2] In contrast to religious practice that is motivated by fear, guilt, and a sense of distance between ourselves and God, creation-centered spirituality acknowledges that Spirit lives within us and expresses Itself *as* us. Some of the most powerful prayers of the creatively spiritual person are happiness, joy, song, laughter, and the appreciative vision of nature as an expression of God's love.

I think Matthew Fox is on to something. God wants us to be happy now. Church is wherever hearts are joyful. Wherever people sing together, God is being glorified and a powerful prayer is touching heaven. Laughter brings healing to our spirit. Whenever someone loves, God is present on earth.

Perhaps the lady who wrote me that note was saying more than I realized. Perhaps as we learn to love ourselves, we gain the courage to sing, love, and laugh wherever we go, and thus bring church with us everywhere. On earth, as it is in heaven.

# I ALREADY
# DID THAT

*It takes a lot of courage to release the familiar,
and seemingly secure, to embrace the new.
But there is no real security in what is no
longer meaningful. There is more security
in the adventurous and exciting, for
in movement there is life, and
in change there is power.*

I was sitting in a parking lot having a philosophical discussion with my little guru, Shanera. We often advise each other on matters of great importance. (Actually, it is usually she who advises me.)

Shanera's sixth birthday was approaching, and I was wishing she could just stay five forever. It seemed as if God had taken everything that is wonderful, witty, and cute, and baked it in this sweet little cake.

"How 'bout if you just stay five, Shanera?" I quipped. "You're so perfect just as you are."

"But that's not how life is!" Shanera giggled. "Life is when you go from five to six...and then seven...and then eight," she explained to me. "Why don't you just let life be the way it is?"

Oh.

I think the kid was reminding me of something I had forgotten. Life is about going from five to six, from thirty-nine to forty, from the old and complete to the new and more exciting.

Beverly Sills, considered by many to be one of the greatest opera singers in American history, recently retired from the stage to become a director. Many people questioned her change of direction, feeling that she still had a great singing career ahead of her. Beverly now wears a gold chain around her neck inscribed with four letters: *"I.A.D.T."* When friends ask her why she stopped singing, Beverly holds up her necklace and explains, *"I Already Did That."*

It takes a lot of courage to release the familiar, and seemingly secure, to embrace the new. But there is no real security in what is no longer meaningful. Ironically, there is more security in the adventurous and exciting, for in movement there is life, and in change there is power. We are only truly secure when we are feeling alive. As Helen Keller said, "Life is a daring adventure—or nothing." Another teacher explained, "A ship in a harbor is safe—but that is not what ships are for." And we are reminded to behold the turtle who makes progress only when he is willing to stick his neck out.

Barry and Joyce Vissell, noted counselors on relationships and parenting, have written a book called *Risk to be Healed.*[3] When you are feeling at risk, you are at your point of power. To step ahead will give you greater strength and wisdom. To stay behind will only delay your journey to becoming yourself.

As I look back upon the significant steps in my life, I see that

I usually felt a sense of risk when I was about to undergo an important change. Now I see that there was never a real risk at all. What I risked losing was my sense of fear and limitation, and the feeling of security in who I believed I was—even if that identity was tiny compared to who I became when I was willing to move forward. When we live in the presence of God, we can laugh at the idea of risk.

Jesus, for example, was one who was fully willing to release the old in order to be empowered by the new. He was not bound by ritual, tradition, or mass thinking. As a child of God, he was subject only to the laws of love, healing, and creativity. Thus he can rightfully be called the Son of God.

We, too, can let go of the laws we believe bind us, and know ourselves to be subject only to the laws of a loving God. We may also rightfully call ourselves Children of God. Jesus was not a special exception to life, bestowed with powers and potentials greater than the rest of us. Jesus was our elder brother, who came to remind us of who we really are. If there is any difference between Jesus and us, it is not one of ability, but awareness. We are equal to Jesus in nature and potential, and now we are ready to join him in equal expression.

Our mission is to accept our Christed nature. Our point of power is to find the light within ourselves and illuminate the world from inside out. The Second Coming is within you. You must know *without a doubt* that you *already* are all that you wish to attract to you. You must acknowledge your divinity and let all else go.

The insightful minister, Eric Butterworth, says that each New Year's he goes through his closet and gives away any clothing or items that he has not used during the past year. This releasing of the old and unnecessary, Eric explains, makes way for the new, the greater, and the better.

This process is a perfect metaphor for an enlightened and enlivened attitude for a new year (which begins at any time we are ready). If we want our good to come to us, we must give it space to enter into our life. In many ways we have made our lives a foolish game of musical chairs in which we offer peace less room than it requires. If we give peace even a little space, it will gently flow to us, permeating our life like fragrant incense wafting through a crack in the door. Just consider how much love we could enjoy if we opened the door fully!

In *Tales of a Magic Monastery,*[4] Brother Theophane tells how he learned to write his own Bible.

> *The first time I went* [to the Magic Monastery] *I forgot to bring my Bible. When I asked the guestmaster if I could borrow a Bible, he said, "Wouldn't you care to write your own?"*
>
> *"What do you mean?"*
>
> *"Well, write your own Bible—something of your own on the order of the Bible. You could tell of a classical bondage and the great liberation, a promised land, sacred songs, a Messiah—that kind of thing. Ought to be much more interesting than just reading some-one else's Bible. And you might learn more."*
>
> *Well, I set to work. It took me a month. I never learned so much about the official Bible. When I was finished, he recommended I take it home and try to live according to it for a year. I should keep a journal of my experience but I shouldn't tell anybody about the project, nor show anyone the book. Next year, after Christmas, I could come back for another retreat.*
>
> *It was quite a year. An eyeopener. Most certainly I had never put so much energy and alertness into living by the official Bible as I was putting into living by this one. And my daily meditations had never been so concentrated.*
>
> *When I arrived back from my next retreat, he greeted me very warmly, took into his hands my Bible and my journal, kissed them with greatest reverence, and told me I could now spend a couple days and nights in the Hall of the Great Fire. On the last night of the year, I should consign my two books to the flames. And that's what I did. A whole year's wisdom and labor—into the Great Fire. Afterwards he set me to work writing another Bible.*
>
> *And so it went, these past forty years. Each year a new Bible, a new journal, and then at the end of the year—into the flames.*

Like Brother Theophane, I have been greatly empowered by casting the old Bibles that I have written into the flames. Not physical Bibles, with pages and print, but the belief systems which have outgrown their service to my growth.

There are two ways in which any path we walk upon strengthens us: Once, when we commit ourselves to it; and again, when we choose to leave it. We build rafts to carry us from one side of a river to the other. To attempt to carry the raft on the next footpath would be self-defeating. Spiritual wisdom is simply knowing when to build the raft, and when to leave it behind.

# NEAR-LIFE
# EXPERIENCES

*Rumor has it that there are a number of
people now walking the earth who have
crossed the threshold and seen what it
would actually be like to be alive.*

A great deal of attention has been paid in recent years to near-death experiences. Nearly all of us are familiar with a book or article about the phenomenon of out-of-body experiences. Perhaps we even know someone who has temporarily crossed the threshold of death and returned to tell about it.

Best-selling books have described these experiences in detail, major motion pictures have dramatized them, and laboratories and institutes have been erected to document them. Let's face it: near-death experiences have become trendy. It has become "in" to be out.

In fact, there has been such glamour associated with being "out," I feel compelled to speak for the "in" crowd. I have been inspired to set up my own research institute: I am studying people who have come very close to living. Rumor has it that there are a number of people now walking the earth who have crossed the threshold and seen what it would actually be like to be alive. I want to meet these people, find out who they are, learn how they think and feel, and discover what it is that would actually cause someone to be happy while in a body. Who knows, I might even be one of them!

The core of this research will be the study of a rarely acknowledged yet apparently common phenomenon called "I.B.E.": "*In- Body Experiences.*" (The abbreviation is pronounced "I Be.") Although we know it will be difficult to find subjects who are not walk-ins, walk-outs, extraterrestrials, U.F.O. abductees, discarnate entities, or reincarnations of Cleopatra, we do expect to find at least a small group of people who have seen God with their eyes open.

The Institute will boldly put aside the age-old question, "Is there life after death?" and seek an answer to the even more pressing need to know, "Is there life *before* death?"

I am happy to report that one study in that field of inquiry has already been completed. When a group of 37 adults were unable to answer the question under laboratory conditions, a field study team journeyed to a local neighborhood playground. There they asked a group of three children if they believed in life before death. The first child replied, "What's death?" The second child laughed, and the third took the researcher by the hand and invited him onto the ballfield. The field study team truly did end up in the field.

The second phase of the Institute's disciplines is based on a study of the life of Bear Bryant. Bear Bryant was the winningest coach in college football history. As the long-time leader of the Alabama football team, Bear accomplished what no other coach has ever been able to do. The Institute wanted to know what made Bear Bryant and his team such grand winners.

Football experts have told us that Coach Bryant showed his team movies of their greatest plays—never their disasters. While other coaches sat their teams down and showed them where they had failed, Bear Bryant continually focused his team's attention on their shining moments. The net result was that other teams created more disasters, while the Alabama team just kept winning. Maybe there is something to looking at the good here on earth, and the part that we play in creating it.

Word has recently reached the Institute that reverence for near-life experiences as we currently know them goes back to the 1950's. It was then that a psychologist named Abraham Maslow began to rethink the training he had received. Dr. Maslow was trying to figure out what makes people healthy psychologically, emotionally, and spiritually.

When Dr. Maslow considered what he had been taught in the classroom, he realized that almost all the models of health that he had seen were based on the study of sick people. Then he had an astounding idea: If we want to learn how to be healthy, why not study healthy people? The idea was simple, powerful, and almost universally overlooked. Dr. Maslow began to study people who were functioning in happy, healthy, and successful ways.

After extensive inquiry, Dr. Maslow discovered that nearly all of the healthy people he studied had had what he called "peak experiences"—moments or periods when they felt exhilarated by life, in love with someone or something; they felt enthusiastic about their ideas or their creative expressions; and they saw purpose and value in being here on earth. Most of these people also felt a strong connection with a spiritual reality—a God, an Essence, a Universal Being—which gave meaning and foundation to their life, and which ultimately brought them real peace.

The net result was that Dr. Maslow quite innocently revolutionized the world of psychology. He, along with a few other visionary thinkers, planted the seeds of the realm that we currently know as humanistic or human potential psychology. This path has shown the healing merits of focusing on what is good, real, and empowering about our lives, and honoring who we are and what we came here to do.

I am happy to announce that the first class sponsored by the Institute will begin soon. The class was inspired by a course description from a popular holistic learning center promising that "this course guarantees you will learn how to get from where you are to where you want to be." With just a slight variation on theme, the Institute's course guarantees that "you will learn how to get from where you want to be to where you are."

Who knows, it could be a veritable phenomenon! People walking the earth who really want to be here, and really are. Who knows, maybe even people like you and me. Who knows? Maybe as a result of reading this account, even more people will come forth with true accounts of near-life experiences. If you happen to be one of them, please let me know.

# Section Two

# *How Angels Fly*

# HOW ANGELS FLY

*Struggle is a sure sign that you are moving against your blessings. Quit fighting for or against your good—it will come to you more quickly when you are relaxed. You cannot fight for peace; if you are fighting for anything, you are at war. Peace is a natural gift that you accept by opening your heart and letting go of the struggle.*

I nspiration comes to me in the most amazing ways. While some people believe that God is present only in the cathedral or the ashram, I have found that the voice of Spirit is quite willing to speak to me on the freeway, in the shower, and in the monastic sanctuary of the toilet. One mystic described God as "a circle whose center is everywhere and whose circumference is nowhere."

God's answer is usually the simplest one. Peace is born of clarity, innocence, and the freedom of an uncluttered mind. By contrast, the way of fear is always complex: We are guilty until proven innocent, and healing is always somewhere around the next bend.

These are not the attributes of the God that I know. The God who has lifted my heart from fear to celebration is a light-hearted friend who always bestows a blessing where I was seeing difficulty. The exit from pain is through the door of the heart.

Happiness is reached by taking gentle steps. I would like to share with you some of the steps I have taken. I am happy to report that these wings of freedom have helped me to fly close to the heart of God. I offer them to you with the vision that we can fly home together. God wants us to be happy.

### 1. Love It All.

The Law of Love is founded on one basic truth: There is one power in the universe, and that power is love. Love is of God and is the same as God. God has no attributes in conflict with love, and is incapable of any action other than love.

There is no force in the universe opposing God, for there is no power outside of the One who created all things in the image and likeness of love. Any evil that we see is nothing more than a concept we hold in our mind. The healing of evil is accomplished not by overcoming or annihilating a force or entity with power, but by choosing to see life through the eyes of love rather than fear.

The process of lifting our vision to see with God is the most exciting and rewarding adventure of life. There is no goal, no quest, and no purpose more real and valuable than the odyssey of transforming our minds to find only love wherever we look.

Let me illustrate. One day I took an excursion with some friends into a Hawaiian bamboo forest. We hiked through the tall, thick bamboo stalks, pausing every few minutes to listen to the sound of the reeds high above us crackling in the wind. After an exciting trek through sparkling mountain streams and lush valleys, we found ourselves at a waterfall hidden in the heart of the Maui mountains. There we swam in the pool, played, and enjoyed a picnic together.

A few people in our group left early that afternoon to attend a meeting in town. We bade them "aloha" and blessed them as they set off to wind their way back through the forest to the road where we had left our cars.

The next day I saw my friend Suzi, one of the women who had left early. I asked her how the meeting went.

"Oh," she laughed, "—we never made it!"

"What happened?"

"Would you believe we got lost in the bamboo forest?"

Sure I would. "That's too bad," I offered. "I'm sorry you missed your meeting."

"Oh, no!" Suzi responded. "It actually turned out better than I ever could have planned—I had a wonderful miracle and healing along the way."

"How so?" I asked.

"On our way back, we discovered that we were not on the trail that we had come in on. We felt lost. One of the women in our group began to feel nervous. As our search for the right trail went on and we did not seem to be getting anywhere, she became very upset. She began to make negative comments and then broke into tears.

"The miracle for me was how I learned to be with her. At first I felt annoyed. I wished that she would be more positive and work with us to find our way home. As she became more and more nervous, I got irked. I wanted support to get out of the forest; instead I felt like I had to take care of a child—and I didn't like it.

"Then I considered that this might be a lesson for me, a teaching in how to handle negativity. Thinking about it in this way, I saw her nervousness not as a problem or an attack, but as a call for love. The little girl within her felt lost and scared. I could certainly identify with that—I have felt that way plenty of times. As my heart opened to her, I saw that her upset was not a burden, but a call for attention. From that point on, I began to give her comfort and encouragement rather than argument or criticism.

"The miracle was that as soon as I started supporting her, we found our way. Quickly we discovered the right path, and before long we were out of the forest. I thought it was interesting that as soon as I found the inner path, the outer path showed up.

"I learned a great lesson that day. I discovered that people around me who are acting negative are not burdens, but opportunities to heal my own consciousness by giving more love. And I am learning compassion for myself as I realize that anyone who bothers me is actually reflecting a part of myself that I haven't come to terms with. So, you see, I received *much* better lessons than I would have at the meeting. The meeting was something I can do any time—the experience in the bamboo forest is a gift that I will cherish forever."

Suzi's experience and the lessons she drew from it were a great example to me. There is nothing outside God's loving plan for our healing. Difficult experiences are especially fruitful, for behind the facade of darkness there is always a shining gift. Love it all. And be sure to make no exceptions to this opportunity for healing.

### 2. *Hang Loose.*
Here are four words that will change your life, if you practice them:

*Let it be easy.*

When I feel a sense of struggle or pressure which is moving me to step out of peace, I hear an inner voice ask, *"How would you be seeing or doing this differently if you were willing to let it be easy?"* As I consider an easier way to approach the situation, a sense of peace and freedom comes over me. From this perspective I can usually see the way out.

Many of us have been imprinted with the belief that life is a struggle, that we have to work to earn love and support, and that suffering and sacrifice buy happiness. *None of this is true.* The glory of life is to live in graceful celebration. *The love of God is a total gift without charge.* To enjoy peace requires no loss whatsoever.

When Albert Einstein was asked, "What is the most important question facing humankind today?" he answered: "Is the universe a friendly place?" It is.

Our sense of struggle can be symbolized by the dilemma of a friend

JOY IS MY COMPASS

of mine who was late for an appointment. As she was speeding on the highway enroute to her meeting, she found herself behind a slow-moving car. Frantically she beeped, tooted, and high-beamed the transgressor in front of her. Finally my friend found a clearing, floored the accelerator, and sped past her adversary. As she turned to look at the driver of the other car, she saw that it was the woman she was speeding to meet.

Hang loose. The struggle is not worth it. Anxious flailing has no purpose or benefit. Life is here to be enjoyed. You cannot be struggling and peaceful at the same time. (As the bumper sticker declares, "You cannot simultaneously call for peace and prepare for war.") Struggle is a sure sign that you are moving against your blessings. Quit fighting for or against your good—it will come to you more quickly when you are relaxed. Peace is not a victory that you can win by battle. You cannot fight for peace; if you are fighting for anything, you are at war. Peace is a natural gift that you accept by opening your heart and letting go of the struggle.

### 3. Be Outrageous.

Blowing a few minds now and then is a very healthy thing to do. It will keep you young and attract friends who enjoy the element of surprise. Remember the words of Saint Ignatius: "The glory of God is humankind fully alive." There is no greater disservice we can do to our friends than to agree with their limitations, and no greater blessing we can bring them than to live in a way that demonstrates that we are free to be whoever we are in the way we joyfully choose.

At one of my weekend retreats I was in a mischievously creative mood. I had a sneaky inspiration that offered me a chance to break out of my sense of self-consciousness and surprise a few people (including myself!) in the process.

It happened at a retreat held around Halloween. One evening we had a "Come As You Were" Reincarnation Ball. All the participants were asked to bring a costume depicting one of their previous lives. For the evening program everyone got together with others with whom they felt they had shared previous lives, and the groups performed skits based on those lives. It was quite an event!

The next morning, as I was getting dressed for the final program of the weekend, I had a positively devilish idea. I remembered that one of the women had worn a beautiful angel costume at the ball. The dainty outfit was built around a long white flowing gown, and it was delightfully angelic. I asked the owner if I could borrow her costume. When I told her what I wanted it for, she was tickled to oblige. I put the angel costume on under my clothes and went to the workshop.

It had been a deeply intimate retreat. Many of the participants had shared important feelings and experiences that had affected their lives in significant ways. Much healing had occurred through this courageous process of self-disclosure.

I stood on the stage before the group of over a hundred retreatants, and took a deep breath. I took the microphone and spoke to the group in a somber voice:

"My friends, there is something I need to tell you, something very important to me."

The room became still. Everyone was waiting to hear what I had to say. I had their attention.

"Many of you have shared deeply this weekend. You have revealed some of the most difficult parts of your life in order to be healed. You have made very powerful and poignant contributions to the retreat, and I thank you for it.

"Now I, too, must share myself without hiding. There is something about me that many of you do not know, even those of you who feel that you know me well. But I can go on no longer without letting you see and know the real me. I must reveal who I truly am."

Now I *really* had their attention. The audience was on the edge of their seats. "What is he going to say?" they all wondered. "Is he going to reveal that he is gay? Or alcoholic? Maybe he's living a double life of some kind!" The soaps had nothing on that moment.

I turned to the piano player at my left. (I had arranged the program with him beforehand.) "Maestro, if you please..."

The maestro was a professional honky-tonk piano player. On cue he went into one of his sassiest striptease rags. Now I had their *total* attention. No one dared leave the room.

I kicked off my shoes (loafers, no less). They sailed into the stage wings. I slinked into my version of bumps and grinds. I had definitely gone over the edge of anything I had done before.

The audience went wild. If nothing else important happened that weekend, they were certainly getting their money's worth at this show.

Some of them considered me a guru or spiritual teacher (these people were among the most confused in the room). This discourse was moving into explicitly uncharted territory.

I went bumping and grinding my way around the stage for a few more bars, and then the critical moment came. As sensuously as I could, I dropped my trousers. That brought a wave of howls. What the howlers didn't expect, however, was that my fallen jeans would reveal the long white skirt of the angel's costume.

"My God, he's a transvestite!" several spectators gasped.

It was working. The beat went on. By now the entire house was up on its feet, clapping and swaying to the honky-tonk beat. It was a classic scene.

Various other articles of clothing fell away. I reached for the buttons of my shirt, under which were stuffed a pair of large gossamer angel wings. I tore off the shirt, and out popped two beautiful wings.

Another gasp rippled through the room. Then laughter and delight.

Soon the entire angel was revealed. For the final touch I donned a sweet little crown, and then blessed the audience with a heavenly wand. As soon as I took up the wand, a harpist began to play etheric strains on his instrument. To this celestial accompaniment I moved from side to side onstage, tapping the retreatants on their third eyes.

When the uproar and applause died down, I took the microphone again and explained, "I told you I wanted to reveal my true identity. I am a being of angelic light, and so are you. If this doesn't prove it, nothing does!"

Everyone cheered. They loved the show and the message. Beyond that, I felt lighter, freer, and more alive—like the angel. I had broken free of the limiting shackles of self-consciousness, and had some fun with my friends and the truth.

To this day, that morning's performance is still talked about by those retreatants. Although the show was years ago, people still ask me if we'll have a striptease at this year's retreat. "Probably not," I tell them. "Let's see what the Holy Spirit has in store for this year."

*Love it all. Hang loose. Be outrageous.* The God I know loves a joyful, open heart, and She has a sense of humor. Remember: Angels can fly because they take themselves lightly.

# THE GIFT
# I BRING YOU

*I need to hold a great vision of who I am
and who my friends are—a vision that is
bigger than what we think we can't do.
There is nothing we can't do.*

I finally made it to Disneyland. After years of cartoons, coonskin caps, and a classic crush on Annette Funicello, I found myself excitedly walking through the gates of Mickey's mecca. The archway over the ticket booths proclaimed it to be "The Happiest Place on Earth." Perhaps it is so.

The family of little girls I was accompanying guided me to all the best attractions, such as Snow White's grotto, Alice in Wonderland's teacup whirl, and the underground pirate boat ride. (I was enthralled, and began to wonder who was chaperoning who!)

When we reached Frontierland, we had a bit of controversy at the gate of the Thunder Mountain roller coaster. Four-year-old Catherine wanted to go on the ride, but her older sister Michelle objected. "It's too scary for you, Catherine," Michelle warned. "The train goes up and down in the dark, and you'll probably cry and want to get off, and you won't be able to."

"I don't care—I want to go anyway!" Catherine insisted.

Frustrated, Michelle turned to me. "I really don't think you should let her go!" the elder sister urged.

I realized I would have to make a decision, and I did not relish the position I was in. Here was a challenge for me. Do I protect the child from a danger she is unaware of, or do I let her choose and learn for herself? I needed help. I remembered a lesson from A Course in Miracles:[5] "Do not teach your brother that he is anything you would not want to be." Hmmm. I did not want to make Catherine small by seeing her as unable to do something she thought she could do. I know the power of vision, and I wanted to affirm Catherine's strength, not her weakness. But I did not want the child to get in over her head. The worst that could happen, I figured, would be that she would feel afraid and cry. The best that could happen would be that she would demonstrate that she was bigger than her sister saw her as being. I decided to make Catherine great by honoring her power to choose.

"Catherine," I began in as honest a way as I could, "I know you want to go on this ride, and you believe that you can. You might really enjoy yourself, and you may also become afraid on the bumps in the dark. You might want to get off before you can. If you understand this, and still want to go, I will let you."

"I want to go!" Catherine declared without hesitation.

"OK," I answered,"—then go for it."

Michelle gave me an "I-sure-hope-you-know-what-you're-doing" look as she took Catherine's hand and stepped toward the gate. I wasn't certain that I was taking the correct action, but it was the best hunch I had to go on.

As I stood by the fence with two-year-old Dawn, I wondered if I had made the right decision. What if Catherine had a terrible experience and became emotionally scarred? What if I had let her parents down by not protecting their child? What if...? But then, I thought, "What if?" is the devil's mantra. The decision was made. I prayed it was the right one.

Twenty minutes later the girls came running off the ride. Catherine had a huge smile on her face. "I did it!" she exclaimed. "I had a great time!" I picked Catherine up in my arms, hugged her tight, and kissed her on the forehead.

"Catherine—that's wonderful!" I told her. "I'm so proud of you! You knew what you could do, and you did it!" She looked up at me and giggled.

I turned to Michelle. She looked surprised and proud. Her sister's success made her bigger, too. Perhaps next time she faced a fear of her own, she would have more courage to overcome it.

What power there is in letting someone be big! I realized that I need to put that same confidence into action with adults, with myself, with everyone. I learned that I need to hold a great vision of who I am and who my friends are—a vision that is bigger than what we think we can't do. There is *nothing* we can't do. *"Try me and prove me,"* says God. It's in the Bible. And it works at Disneyland.

That day we also saw *Captain EO,* a marvelous metaphysical musical, the offspring of the creative marriage of Disney and George Lucas of *Star Wars* fame. The movie is a 3D lesson in the power of vision, starring Michael Jackson as Captain EO, who teaches us how to overlook limitations and see only truth.

Captain EO is sent to liberate a planet enslaved by an evil witch. Boldly the captain breakdances into the witch's headquarters and informs her, "I have a gift for you!"

"What gift could you have for me?" the witch-queen cackles. She extends her 3D fingernails into the audience, and all the kids in the theatre (including me) squirm back in our seats. Those nails sure look real!

"The gift I bring you is yourself," Captain EO firmly announces. His eyes are piercing; I feel his power.

"That's no gift!" she declares. "I belong to the darkness."

The captain is not intimidated. "But that is not your true self," the valiant EO proclaims. "There is something inside you which is much more beautiful than the one you appear to be. I have come to show you who you really are!"

With this bold assertion, the good captain extends his arm, opens his hand, and surges a beam of golden light toward one of the queen's guards. The light penetrates the guard, and instantly his armor explodes and drops away.

The queen hisses. Her fearful belief system is threatened, and she senses that her dark empire is about to be dissolved. Fear does not readily give way to love.

But there is really no contest. Captain EO goes on to zap the rest of the witch's guards. One by one they emerge as radiant young men and women. Quickly these transformed beings spring to the center of the great hall, where they join Captain EO in some very slick moon-walks and snappy moves that clearly bear the Michael Jackson trademark. Together they sing, *"We can change the world!"*

Captain EO turns to the queen. He raises his hand and beams her a laser of light that no darkness could resist. Instantly her cloak and fingernails are blown away, and there, where darkness once dominated, stands a luminous and elegant princess of light. She joins the dance, and together they whip up a storm of energy which the Captain rides off the planet. Michael throws in a few wiggles on his way out.

The audience applauds wildly. The lights come on, and as the music continues we all bop our way out the exit doors, depositing our 3D glasses in the appropriate bin. As I step into the daylight I find myself on one of the streets of Tomorrowland. I begin to feel that I've seen more than a movie. I have the distinct sense that once again I have been taught the lesson of the ages. (It keeps appearing on different stages.)

I am reminded that there is no greater gift we can bestow upon friends than to let them be big, to see the greatness in them when they or the world would acknowledge only their smallness. I call it divine x-ray vision—seeing ourselves and one another as God sees us. When we look at ourselves and our life through divine eyes, we see the truth

43

about our possibilities. Tunnel vision, on the other hand, shows us only a small portion of who we truly are. We must choose which kind
of sight we would use.

At the end of our day at Disneyland our little troupe sat under a
tree and relaxed, laughing about our adventure. "What do you think
the letters in Captain *EO* stand for?" one of the children wondered. We
all began to guess. No one seemed to be able to figure it out.

"I know!" a little one called out, her face aglow. "Captain *EO* stands
for *EveryOne!*"

Frontierland . . . Adventureland . . . Tomorrowland. "The
happiest place on earth." Hmmmm. Maybe Walt was on to something.

# HOME FOR
# THE HOLIDAYS

*I began to consider my life, and how I
approach my activities. I thought about
the times I feel a sense of struggle, trying
to force the universe to behave the way I think
it should. Then, sooner or later I realize
that I would rather have peace.*

Waipoli Drive is a magnificent panoramic road winding its way down the western slopes of Mount Haleakala on the island of Maui. From certain points on this ribbon road, one can gaze out over the entire central valley of the island and behold a shimmering sea of sugar cane waving in the tradewinds like emerald reeds in the South Pacific sunlight. From this vantage point I sense how the ancient Hawaiians felt to look upon the riches of God's creation. Spirit is very present here.

One morning while driving down this magical road, I saw a man at peace. He was not an ancient *kahuna* priest or a meditating yogi. Nor was he a teacher of metaphysics. This man of peace was simply flying a toy glider. As I watched the glider soar back and forth across the powder blue sky, I became mesmerized. Rarely have I seen a dance so reminiscent of ease and freedom. Gently, lightly, the tiny craft floated over the meadows, relying on nothing but the wispy breeze to hold it aloft. It was the picture of effortless life—movement without struggle, expression without striving.

I pulled my car off the road and turned off the motor. I looked up to the top of the hill and saw that the pilot was controlling the vessel's movements with a small radio transmitter. The man was still, maneuvering the plane from a hundred yards' distance with but a small turn of his wrist. On this sunny Saturday morning he had driven up from the valley, leaving everything behind to watch poetry in flight. I sat and watched for a long time. The music on my cassette player poured forth, lofty and inspiring. This moment was clearly orchestrated for joy.

I began to consider my life, and how I approach my activities. I thought about the times I feel a sense of struggle, trying to force the universe to behave the way I think it should. Sometimes I find myself attempting to manipulate people or events to fit my model of how it should be. Then, sooner or later I realize that I would rather have peace. I release my idea to allow Spirit's idea to be expressed. O, to soar like that glider always! It must be possible.

Donald Shimoda, the colorful reluctant messiah in Richard Bach's *Illusions,*[6] piloted an airplane which bore no dead bugs on the windshield and never tattled of an oil leak. The narrator, Richard, could not understand how Shimoda managed this feat. I know how he did it. He didn't battle with things that bugged him, and he had no slippage in the gears of his mind. He flowed with the currents of life instead of trying to buck them.

As I hold the desire for deeper, richer healing in my life, I know it would do me well to hold that image of the graceful glider close to my heart. Consider the holiday season, for example. What is the use of celebrating a spiritual holiday if we lose our peace in doing so? I think it would be better to have no holiday and be at peace than to lose our joy to insanity. Travel, family gatherings, and exchanging gifts are meaningful only if they are an expression of our love. If what we are doing doesn't bring us joy, we must stop and ask ourselves, "What would I do if I were willing to be true to myself?"

Someone once explained to me the relationship between what happens and happiness. The words *happen* and *happiness* both come from the same root word. We are happy when we allow life to happen. We become unhappy when we resist what is happening. (One of my friends tells me he has recently resigned as General Manager of the Universe, and he is much happier for it! Perhaps we can learn from his choice.)

Sometimes what wants to happen becomes obvious through the voice of another person, and sometimes the flow of life makes itself known from the depths of our own heart. We must honor the voice of truth no matter what messenger brings it to our door.

I feel certain we would be much happier if we allowed the holidays to happen as Spirit guides us rather than trying to bend them to our notions. It is a wise soul who can allow those relatives who want to come for Thanksgiving to come, and allow those relatives who do not want to come, *not* to come.

We might also use the holiday season to practice the highest spiritual path of all—self-appreciation. We might practice honoring who we are, rather than fighting with ourselves to be who we "should" be. This year you might give yourself the gift of doing what you would *like* to do for the holidays, instead of forcing yourself to do what you think you *should* do. For Thanksgiving, be where you would be most thankful to be. For Christmas, let Christ be born in you, rather than a distorted image of what others expect of you. Celebrate New Year's in a way that the year becomes new because you are becoming more alive. You may discover that the holidays take on an entirely new light. This time let it be easy. Let's come home for the holidays.

# FROM MYSTERY
# TO MASTERY

*When we see choice instead of chance,
we become the creator of our experience,
and we claim our identity as
master of our destiny.*

Why is it that some people are successful at whatever they do, while others seem to continually fail?

A friend of mine, Tolly Burkan, has been successful at many business ventures throughout his life. As a teenager, Tolly learned to be a clown magician. Before long he was a popular entertainer at local parties and hospitals.

Then Tolly took his knowledge of balloon sculpture (French poodles and the like) on the road. He earned a great deal of money while traveling around the world on luxury ocean liners and visiting exotic lands.

Later Tolly went to Ken Keyes' *Living Love Center* in Berkeley, where he was invited to become the training director.

Tolly then went to India, where he watched people walk barefoot over thousand-degree burning coals. "If these people can do that, so can I—and so can anyone!" Tolly reasoned. Soon he had translated his experience into a firewalking workshop which he introduced to America. Ten years later, many thousands of people (including me) have traversed the bed of fire and in the process learned to overcome fear.

Along his way, Tolly has written some successful books and produced a record album of his songs. This achievement is especially impressive to me as I consider that several years earlier Tolly did not believe he was a very good singer. But Tolly kept the spotlight of his attention on mastery.

Tolly's success at whatever he has undertaken cannot be attributed to luck. His success is the product of a mind that is willing to succeed. Though the projects that he was involved in were varied in nature, there was one consistent factor: Tolly *chose to win* at life.

You and I can enjoy the same success by being willing to *own* everything that happens to us as our creation. Complete responsibility for our life may seem frightening at first, but ultimately there is nothing more empowering than knowing that life gives its gifts to those whose arms are open to accept them. With the acceptance of such responsibility comes great freedom, for in it we are united with the Mind that created this garden universe.

"Chance plays no part in God's plan," *A Course in Miracles* tells us. Metaphysicians explain that "accidents do not happen—they are created." Jerry Jampolsky, author of the popular book, *Love is Letting Go of Fear,* says that "a coincidence is a miracle in which God wishes to remain anonymous."

Where and how did we learn to believe there is a force in the universe which operates outside the power of our own being? Surely it must be a projection of a split mind to see a world in which we have only partial power. As Children of an almighty God, we must be heir to *all* our Father's power. To believe that there is any level at which we are not one with God is to cut off a part of ourselves from the light and give darkness unwarranted might. Darkness, like chance, is not real, and therefore has no power.

What we normally attribute to a force called "luck" is simply the part of our mind that does not see the whole picture. No one creates any condition—health, finances, career, relationship—unless she or he has attracted it by patterns of thinking. As a poet said, "We think in secret and it comes to pass; environment is our looking glass."

If we want to change our luck, we must change our patterns of thinking. Just as the waves of the ocean create distinct physical formations of sand and rock on beaches, the waves of our thoughts create physical manifestations in our experience. How powerful is our mind! If we can catch even a glimpse of our identity as the creator of our experience, we are well on our way from mystery to mastery of living, which is the essence of our life as spiritual beings.

### *Programmed to Succeed*

My friend Mildred Potenza is a successful consultant in the field of motivation. When I wished Millie luck at the beginning of a new course she was teaching, she smiled and answered, "Thanks, but I don't need luck—I'm programmed to succeed."

So can we *all* create successful lives. It is not luck that we need, but awareness—the awareness that we can write the script of our movie. We need to quit being an extra in someone else's movie, and become the star of our own.

Let us walk this world in joy! No longer can we believe that we are the effects of a mysterious and capricious cause. We are one with the Cause, Children of a creative God who takes delight in our perfect expressiveness. Power and creativity are one. We are the brightest of ideas in God's creative mind. When we see choice instead of chance, we live in the grace of our own shining self.

# THE INTENTIONAL
# TRAVELER

*Instead of seeing life as a boring responsibility,
we can play it as a romantic adventure.
We came to learn to love more deeply,
feel more fully, give who we are,
and wholeheartedly receive the same.*

It is generally agreed that the worst thing that could happen to someone is death. Yet there is something worse than death, and that is fear of life. In no single moment is death real; every moment we touch is replete with life unless we allow fear to become our master.

I enjoyed the message of the movie, *The Accidental Tourist*. The story is about Macon Leary, who writes travel guides for people who don't like to travel but are forced to because of their occupation. Mr. Leary provides expert advice on how his readers can buffer and protect themselves from unforeseen events.

Mr. Leary's advisories for unwilling travelers include: "Always bring a book on an airplane to protect yourself from people who want to talk to you"; "Wear a grey suit, as it is appropriate for any occasion, including funerals"; and "Take your own laundry soap, so you do not have to depend on other people for such necessities."

Not surprisingly, Macon lives his entire personal life as an unwilling traveler. After the sudden death of his twelve-year-old son, Macon and his family closed down their hearts and began to build thick walls to shield themselves from pain—walls as grey as the suits he prescribes.

Macon's family is so afraid of life that they do not answer the telephone, they turn down friendships point blank, and their big thrill of the week is to alphabetize the groceries as they stack the pantry shelf. This family lends new meaning to the word "protected"; they are a sort of despondent version of the Munsters.

But then, as fate—or "accident," as the movie terms it—would have it, Macon is confronted with the romantic advances of a young woman as kooky as he is boring. These two are perfectly the opposite: She is irresistibly forthright, while he is immovably resistant—a match made in heaven, to be sure!

And as with other couples it joins, heaven would have its way with this one. When Macon goes home to meet the woman's son, his heart is touched. He remembers that the joy of feeling love outshines the seeming value of isolation. While his "accidental" encounter with this woman was at first a nuisance, it ultimately becomes his salvation.

I could see some of myself in Macon Leary. I look at the ways I have shielded myself from life. When the fire in an intimate relationship got too hot, I would escape to another relationship. When I felt lost or uncertain, I hid in my office work. I put off challenging decisions in favor of easy ones. I denied my feelings to myself and my friends. I have *been* Mr. Leary.

Yet there is another way of looking at things, as there always is. There is a way to master life—not by running away from it, but by diving into it. Instead of seeing life as a boring responsibility, we can play it as a romantic adventure. Even if we have chosen incorrectly in the past, we can choose again now.

### *From Irritation to Elation*

Let me share with you an experience I had in learning to choose happiness. Recently I purchased a hot tub. It took a bit of arranging to buy the spa in California and have it shipped to my home in Hawaii. A friend offered to pick up the unit at the dock and unload it at the site in my backyard.

When the spa arrived, we realized it would be quite a project to unload the 1,000-pound unit and move it from the pickup truck down the hill to the site. Our carpenter rigged up a makeshift ramp, and we called five of our friends to help move the hot tub. As we began to dislodge the crate from the truck, we noticed that the truck was parked unevenly on the side of the hill. Then we realized that we were standing on the downhill side of the truck. If the big box slipped, we would be beneath it. We started to move the box, and it began to slide in our direction.

We stopped to reconsider our strategy. (We all like pancakes, but we didn't feature becoming a short stack!) As often happens in committees, everyone had their opinion on how to move it. We heard every idea from "We better get a fork lift" to "Come on, let's just do it." Sometimes it seemed like there were more opinions than people present.

I began to feel irritated. "This is a big nuisance," I told myself. "I should never have gotten into this...I should have bought a spa locally...I'm never going to do anything like this again..." and so on. I began to feel like an accidental tourist, burdened and obligated by the pressures of life, a victim of forces beyond my control. I was seeking to withdraw from the challenge rather than master it.

When I recognized the downward spiralling path my mind was taking me on, I didn't like it. "Is this the way you really want to think?" I asked myself. No, of course it wasn't.

"How might I see this differently?" I wondered. Then the word *adventure* came to me. "That's it—this is an adventure!" I lit up. This challenge did not need to be a fearful hardship; seen from another viewing point, it could be an exciting odyssey. Here I was with five good friends, playing together on the crest of a beautiful Hawaiian valley on a warm and sunny day. I pictured a time in the future when we would look back on the morning we moved the hot tub, and we would have a good laugh.

Then I thought about having that laugh while stretched out in the warm bubbling waters of the spa. That was the ticket! I remembered the vision, why we were doing this. There was a purpose, a higher goal than just to move a big heavy box.

Then the project became fun. We made some adjustments to the ramp and tried again. To our delight, down slid the big crate, as if it was greased and guided by an unseen hand. (Perhaps it was!) Within minutes the spa was positioned on its pad. We all shook hands and hugged.

The spa was installed, but along with it there was an installation that was even more important. It was a change in my mind, the willingness to look at what we were doing in a different light. That made all the difference.

We are not accidental tourists. We are intentional travelers. No one put us here to buffer and suffer. We chose to be here. We came to learn to love more deeply, feel more fully, give who we are, and wholeheartedly receive the same.

Last night we sat in the spa for the first time. After coming home from a few weeks of intense traveling, Karren and I stepped into the hot tub and sat back to relax. I remembered the experience of installing the spa, and how I had lifted myself out of fear and frustration by envisioning the moment I was now enjoying. I laughed. It was all worth it. I was very glad that I had chosen to enjoy the adventure.

# LET IT ALL
# BE GOOD

*We do not become happy because we
get what we want; we get what we
want because we choose happiness first.*

A man walking through a small town in India came upon a sadhu (religious renunciate) sitting by the side of the road. The sadhu was adding a small rock to a pile of stones he had amassed. The passerby's curiosity was aroused. He approached the sadhu and asked what he was doing.

"Do you see that woman entering that house with that man over there?" the sadhu asked.

"Yes," the fellow responded.

"The woman is a prostitute," the sadhu told him. "I have been watching her for a long time. One by one, she attracts men on the street and takes them to her room. For each man she has enticed, I have put a stone on this pile. You can see how big the mound is. Little will be her reward in heaven."

Years passed. The woman fell ill and left this world at a young age. Soon afterward, the sadhu passed as well. When he arrived at heaven's gate, the sadhu was astonished to see the prostitute in heaven, sitting joyfully at the feet of the Lord.

When the sadhu asked to be shown to his place in heaven, he was told that this was as far as he could go. Instead of the golden mansion he expected, the sadhu was given a pile of cold gray rocks. He was told that this was his lot with which to build his home.

"What is this?" the sadhu complained. "That woman in there was a sinner in life, and she sits at the feet of the Lord. I, a religious man of many years, am consigned to a little mound of stones!"

The gatekeeper explained: "Your reward is founded not on the appearance you projected in your life, but by the intention in your heart. The woman you judged hated what she was doing, but she felt that she had to do it. She knew no other way to support herself and her child. While she was with each man you saw, she was praying in her heart, 'Oh, God, please get me out of this—there must be another way!' She was kind and compassionate to the men who came to her, many of whom needed a loving friend more than sex.

"You, on the other hand," the gatekeeper continued, "were steeped in judgment and self-righteousness. While she was calling to the Lord, you were counting her sins with your stones. Now she has received the fruits of her thoughts, and so have you."

Thanksgiving is a precious time of year. It is the time when we consciously join to recognize the good and let the rest go. The holiday *(holy day)* is an outward demonstration of an inner process that brings us great healing. Appreciation is perhaps the quickest and most powerful way to God. Gratitude is the adhesive that draws our good to us and multiplies our happiness as we acknowledge and glorify what we love. Enlightenment is simply substituting God's judgment of life—which is always good—for any thoughts we had to the contrary. It is the healing of our mind, and a giant step on our road home to real peace.

### Choose Happiness First

The Option Process, formulated by Barry Neil and Suzy Lite Kaufman, authors of *Sonrise,*[8] explains that happy people attract what they want in life more often than unhappy people. We do not become happy because we get what we want; we get what we want because we choose happiness first. When we turn our minds and hearts to the loving God within, we draw to us all that is good, healing, and uplifting. "Seek ye first the Kingdom, and all shall be added."

Whenever we hold a judgment, we cut ourselves off from our Source. To offer forgiveness instead of attack is to quickly and consciously reunite our heart with the God we seek. This is how we make way for miracles.

We can look upon our sins or our healing, our frailties or our magnificence, our limitations or our spirit. We cannot see both. And we will receive more of whatever we look upon. Every thought is a prayer, a seed, an investment in more of the same. It is the wise student of truth who chooses to look upon the good and allow the rest to go. "Two men looked out through prison bars. One saw mud; the other, stars."

I am very glad that someone decided to create a holiday called Thanksgiving. It is a time when we can put aside the scurrying about that so often distracts us, and join with our families to remember that the most important thing in life is to be together in spirit. Gratefulness allows us to touch and join in the safe kingdom of the appreciative heart. The attitude of gratitude brings altitude. This Thanksgiving, let's let it all be good, all a gift, all from God. Let's remember that life is not about appearances; it's about the truth of the heart. Most of all, let's celebrate with one another and share this spectacular adventure of finding God everywhere.

# NUDE
# FRONTIERS

*When challenged by pro-garmentites about*
*the Nuddhist's proselytizing activities,*
*Ms. Berry simply responded,*
*"We have nothing to hide."*

As I was sunbathing today, it occurred to me that being naked is a pretty holy experience. We enter this world naked, we leave it naked, and I am wondering where we got the idea that the time in between should be different.

When I spent some time at the Esalen Institute years ago, nudity was a part of the lifestyle there. Personally, I found it rather refreshing. For the first few days my eyes fell below some belly buttons, but after just a short time, walking around with no clothing seemed to be a very natural and innocent way to interact. Whereas one might expect such an atmosphere to be sexually stimulating, I found it to be less provocative than a normally clothed society, in which many styles of clothing are designed to stimulate sexual fantasy by accent and mystery.

In fact, the liberation I felt while sunbathing was an enlightening experience that led me to stumble barefoot upon an ancient lost religion: *Nuddhism.* Nuddhism was founded thousands of years ago by an enlightened being known affectionately to his followers as *the Nuddha.* The Nuddha attained enlightenment while meditating under the Body Tree. He renounced his life as a pelt peddler in the garment district of Calcutta and entered religious life, whereupon he preached at many beaches, health spas, and private homes with high backyard fences. He was especially popular with the poor, since he did not solicit donations at his outdoor services. "He can't pocket your money," missionaries told proselytes.

The Nuddha is the patron saint of hot tubs, deserted swimming holes, and tanning salons. Some of the documented miracles attributed to the Nuddha include distracting police officers en route to certain Southern California beaches, making "jacuzzi" a household word, and helping the backers of the musical *Hair* bring the show to Broadway.

Membership in the order is especially attractive, as the wardrobe budget is very low. There is virtually no hierarchy in the structure of the religion, since the priests cannot be distinguished from the parishioners. The generally free-thinking and non-judgmental attitude of the Nuddhists was established at the inception of the faith when, in the original articles of the religion, the Nuddha declared that this kind of life would not be attractive to clothes-minded people.

Nuddhist practitioners gather together in the morning and meditate on soft blankets in an ancient practice known as "Zenbathing." Meditators are known for their ability to remain very still during their religious services, until the moment a gong is sounded and the assembly rolls over in unison.

Recently there has been a revival of the ancient practices of Nuddhism. A large part of its new-found popularity can be attributed to footprints that have been discovered beneath the sands of the Riviera, where legend has it that the Nuddha walked and left his blessing thousands of years ago. He is reputed to have prophesied, "One day my people will walk topless in the sun." Sure enough, the footsteps of the Nuddha have been followed by millions who want to keep abreast of their religion.

The Nuddhists are now rallying together to support the repair of the ozone layer of the earth's atmosphere. They cite the sun as their friend for centuries, and they are not about to see the sun of God crucified by unconscious aerosol use. In a recent *Eyewitness News* interview investigating the Nuddhists' political action against aerosol manufacturers, Brown S. A. Berry, the Beachchairwoman of the Naked—Not Faked party, cited the movement's inspiring slogan: "It's our can or yours!"

Living in an age of mega-mergers, the Nuddhists have formed partnerships with various other popular groups to inspire clothes-minded people to join their religion and support their cause. They have bought an interest in a pro football team and changed the name to the Chicago Bares; surreptitiously removed millions of jars of bikini wax from retail shelves; and produced thousands of subliminal cassette tapes seeded with the subconscious message, *"Skin is in."* When challenged by pro-garmentites about the religion's proselytizing activities, Ms. Berry simply responded, "We have nothing to hide."

What about the future? The Nuddhists do have a book of rich prophesies. In the sacred *Barefoot Bible* it is foreseen that we are on the threshold of a Nude Age. One day, perhaps even in our lifetime, we will see the birth and dissemination of enlightening magazines such as *Nude Age, Nude Realities,* and *Nude Frontier.* A nude channeler, Bufftha, has explained that certain rudimentary forms of these magazines already exist.

If you would like to explore the practice of Nuddhism, the elders of the religion guarantee that you will see more than you are seeing in your current religion. They expect that you will enjoy the shorter services, since the passing of the offering plate has been entirely eliminated. And they promise you will find a whole new meaning in religion when you give your fellow parishioners the kiss of peace.

# Section Three

# *Going the Distance*

# I MET THE CHRIST TODAY

*I began to consider the situations in my life in which I have invested more in being right than in releasing my brother. I decided that I might do well to forget some of my rules, such as "punishment, pain, or payment due."*

I met the Christ today. He was not preaching on a hillside overlooking Jerusalem. He did not appear in a flash as I was kneeling before the altar of a church. Nor did he speak to my heart in the quietude of meditation.

Today I found the Christ standing behind a ticket counter at the Denver airport. He was not tall of stature, nor was he garbed in a flowing robe. And he did not speak of God by that name. The Christ I met today handled baggage, his skin was black, and his eyes sparkled through wire spectacles. His name was not Jesus, but Joey. And he was every bit as much a savior.

I should have known that my need upon arriving at the airport was an invitation for an angel. Yesterday, at the conclusion of our workshop tour, Karren discovered that she needed to make an unexpected visit to Los Angeles before returning home to Maui. When we looked at her ticket, we were reminded that it was marked *"non-refundable, non-transferable."*

"$200 down the drain," I griped to myself, "...plus the expense of a new ticket to Maui, and an additional fare to Los Angeles." I was not thrilled at the prospect of paying such a high price because the ticket could not be exchanged.

My mind searched for ways around paying the extra money. I considered trying to sell the ticket to someone in the waiting area. I wondered if I should fabricate a juicy story to win the sympathy of the ticket agent. Then I remembered the subtitle of a book that I had just seen, a lesson on integrity in business: *You Don't Have to Cheat to Get What You Want.*[9] Oh, yes.

I decided to let the truth be my friend. I approached the counter and placed the ticket clearly before the agent.

"We're holding this ticket marked 'non-refundable' for Maui today," I told him. "Karren needs to make an unexpected trip to L.A. before going home. Do you have any ideas on what we can do about this?" I watched his face carefully for his expression. I felt as if our fate was in his hands.

"Oh, I imagine I might..." he answered. His eyes lit up with a friendly smile. "Let's take a look..."

He began to type on the computer. As his fingers danced sprily over the keyboard, I watched his face. His eyes studied the screen carefully. He kept working, figuring, probing, searching. My fingers, on the other hand, were crossed. I was asking for a miracle.

"OK," he came back. No readable expression on his face. "This machine here says that the ticket is non-refundable and non-transferable..."

My heart began to sink.

"However, I am not a very good reader, and I see no reason to read that line—especially when it would cost you an additional $431 to get home. So here's what I'm going to do: I'm writing you a free ticket to L.A. That'll handle you for today. When you get to the counter in L.A. on your way home next week, give them your original ticket, act a little crazy, like you don't have the slightest idea what's going on. Tell them that some funny little black dude at the Denver desk said you could use your original ticket home. Most of the agents there will go for it; if they give you a hard time, tell them you think I may have been on drugs."

We laughed. Joey went on, "I don't know why I'm doing this. But what's the use of working here if I can't have some fun? You shouldn't have to pay any more to get home." He handed us the ticket to L.A. and smiled.

As we accepted the ticket, I asked Joey if I could recommend him for sainthood. He laughed. I looked at the long line of passengers waiting behind us, and realized Joey must have spent at least twenty minutes with us playing angel.

"Hey, Joey, are you making a career out of it?" the agent to our left quipped. "If you keep these people at the counter any longer, they'll miss their plane and we'll have to take them to dinner."

"Cool your jets," Joey bounced back. "They're smiling, aren't they?" You bet we were.

Karren hugged Joey. I kissed his hand. We all laughed and said good-bye. He wished us a nice flight. I thought his words were a little redundant.

*"You should show mercy, for only mercy has been shown to you,"* A Course in Miracles advises us. Sitting in the airplane on the way home, I saw Joey's face before me, and I began to weep. He didn't have to do what he did for us. He could have invoked the rules and charged Karren another $431 to get home. But the rules were not as important to him as people. Something in Joey's heart told him that mercy was more meaningful than policy.

I thought of Jesus in Galilee as the townspeople were about to stone the adulterous woman. He told them to forgive her. "But this is the punishment prescribed by law!" the angry people argued. "There is a Higher Law," Jesus reminded them. The master was teaching them that mercy is more important than policy.

I began to consider the situations in my life in which I have invested more in being right than in releasing my brother. I thought of one person who owed me money, and yet had no means to repay. I remembered people who had faltered on jobs they had promised to do for me. I had felt upset with a woman who had promised her heart to me and later turned away. Then I remembered Joey's voice as he told us, "...but I'm not a good reader."

I decided that I might do well to diminish some of my reading skills—especially those which called my attention to edicts like "punishment, pain, or payment due." Joey inspired me to keep passing forgiveness along. Meher Baba taught, "True love is contagious; it goes on gathering force and transforming everyone it touches." *A Course in Miracles* calls forgiveness "the chain of atonement," which has the power to inspire those who receive it to pass it on to others. As I considered the enormity of the gift I had received, I uttered a prayer, "God, please let me grant mercy to others as Joey has shown it to me."

I met the Christ today. I had thought we were stepping up to the ticket counter to buy an airplane ticket. And the counter became an altar. There I found release, awakening, and the gentle gift of those who find solace in the laws of God rather than the limits of the world.

# WHERE
# LOVE WILLS

*Love is indeed the greatest, and the only power in the universe. Where love wills to go, it always finds a way.*

H ave you ever wondered if the love you are giving is being appreciated or acknowledged? Have you ever received a great gift from someone you had lost touch with, and wished you could thank them? Do you wonder how God finds ways to join people who love one another?

I happened upon a most enlightening television program which answered these questions quite clearly for me. It showed me love in action on earth, leaving no doubt in my mind that the will of love always finds a way.

Veteran news commentator Charles Kuralt was presenting a world-class series called *Back on the Road*. Mr. Kuralt, along with just a few video technicians, took to the highways and back roads of America to find unusual people using their lives in meaningful and inspiring ways.

There was a 93-year-old man who has spent 83 of those years making bricks. During all this time he has used only his hands, a prehistoric-looking wooden turnstile tool, and a mule. Charles took a walk with George Black through his little country town where nearly every brick has been formed by this man's strong and graceful hands. George was aglow with pride and satisfaction. He bore the dignity of one whose life has been spent in simplicity and service.

Then there was the fellow who had taken it upon himself to build a state highway. Twelve years earlier he had felt a need for a major thoroughfare between his town and another in the state. Finding the government unwilling to lay down a road, he went ahead and did it himself. He negotiated for land and easements, and with only a shovel, a wheelbarrow, and an ancient John Deere tractor, he set out to bring his vision to life.

To date, he has completed nine miles of the highway. How many to go? 124. Will he ever complete it? Probably not. Then why is he doing it? Because (as Charles Kuralt says he learned from the man) "sometimes the process is more important than the final product."

The most astonishing and moving story in the program was about a Russian man named Alexei. This elderly Soviet showed up at the hotel in Moscow where the CBS news team was staying during the presidential summit talks. After Alexei ardently insisted on seeing an American reporter, Charles Kuralt met with him. Sitting together on a park bench in Moscow, Alexei related his amazing story. Kuralt listened intently, and the video cameras captured the tale:

During World War II, Alexei had been a prisoner of war in a Nazi compound. He, along with a group of Russian soldiers, were held captive in a barbed-wire yard adjacent to a group of American prisoners. The Americans were receiving food through a special airlift program, while the Russians were starving to death with the meager Nazi rations.

Alexei befriended a few of the American soldiers on the other side of the fence, and together they devised a plan whereby the Americans would collect some of their rations and pass them over the fence to the Russians at night. All of the men—Americans and Russians alike—realized that being caught by the Nazis would mean instant death. Yet the power of their willingness to help one another was stronger than their fear.

The plan proceeded successfully, and many Russian lives were saved as a result. The Americans even went so far as to take the bodies of soldiers who had died in their barracks and bring them to roll call. They propped the corpses up in their midst, and when the dead soldiers' names were called, others would answer for them. In this way the Americans were able to obtain more rations, which they shared with the Russians.

The Nazis discovered the secret food-sharing plan, and they called all the Americans into the yard for questioning. Despite brutal Nazi interrogation, not one of the Americans confessed or revealed the identity of anyone participating in the plot. Such was the depth and integrity of the camaraderie that grew from those trying times.

When Alexei was released from the prison camp, he vowed in his heart that one day he would find a way to thank his American friends. Nearly 50 years later, the gratitude in this man's heart moved him to find someone who could deliver his gift of thanks to the rightful recipients. He asked Charles to carry his message to the handful of the Americans with whom he had joined to survive.

The reporter was rapt, as I was. How amazing was this man's determination to share his gratitude! For me, Alexei's story was a demonstration of the power that we all have to help and heal one another when we are willing to see one another as part of our family rather than enemies or strangers.

But there is more. Upon his return to the United States, Mr. Kuralt found the former American soldiers that Alexei named. They bore witness to the accuracy of Alexei's account. Never did they expect to hear from him again; they were not even sure if Alexei had lived. And now to receive a message of thanks from him! They were touched beyond measure.

The next scene of the documentary showed these men on the telephone to Alexei, weeping and speaking the little Russian they remembered. These retired military men became vulnerable little boys as they recalled their painful yet heartful time in the prison camp. They had no idea this day would ever come.

As if that were not enough of a heart-mover, we then saw the former American soldiers and their families arriving at the train station in Moscow. There was Alexei waiting for them with open arms. The men fell into each other's arms and wept openly. And I wept with them.

Truly there is a God of love, One who bears the power to express the heart's deepest yearnings, especially when we aspire to give love. As I consider the gifts and miracles that worked through everyone involved in this astounding story—Alexei, all the Russians and Americans in the prison camp, the CBS news team, and all of us who viewed the tale—I cannot help but feel a deep knowing that love is indeed the greatest, and the only power in the universe. Where love wills to go, it always finds a way.

# X-RAY
# VISION

*Your success depends entirely on the vision you choose to employ. You can see either perfection or problems; there is no in-between. Remember this, and you will be unlimited in your ability to heal.*

"I don't want to treat this man," the doctor thought to himself. Though he would not say it aloud, he was having a very hard time being with this patient.

The man had entered Nelson Decker's chiropractic office in Englewood, New Jersey, and requested free service, as he had no money to pay. Dr. Decker had offered service without charge before, but this man was tougher to deal with. He was dirty, unkempt, and emitted a strong body odor. The doctor wondered when the man had last had a bath.

"How can I treat this man?" he wondered.

Then Nelson remembered years before, when he had studied healing with some Native American teachers. One of the elders had told him, "If you want to be a real healer, find something you honestly like in every situation." *Honestly* was the key word here.

"What can I honestly say I like about this man?" the doctor wondered. There wasn't much. He scanned the fellow from head to toe. Finally he noticed that the man's shoelaces were tied neatly. Being a rather tidy fellow himself, Nelson appreciated that even though this fellow was in a state of dishevelment, his shoes were laced in an orderly fashion.

At that moment something happened in Dr. Decker's heart. He felt an opening; it was as if he had discovered a door in a room that at first appeared totally bounded by walls. He felt that on some level—even if it did not seem to be a very important one—he was joined with this man who had first seemed to be so different. Nelson had broken through the membrane of his sense of separation and opened a crack in the door to healing. A feeling of peace and relief began to flow through his body. With this newfound sense of respect, he willingly treated the man. The fellow thanked him and left the office.

About a week later the same fellow returned. This time he looked much better. He was clean, dressed more neatly, and his body odor was gone. The doctor was pleased to see this transformation in such a short time.

The fellow approached Nelson and took his hand. "Dr. Decker," he began, "I want to thank you for saving my life."

"What do you mean?" the physician responded. "I didn't know you had a life-threatening illness."

"When I walked through your door last week, I was in the pits of my life," the man explained. "Everything had fallen apart, and I had been wandering the streets of New York City for I don't know how long. I decided that I could go on no longer. I made my way to the George Washington Bridge, where I fully intended to jump to oblivion.

"As I approached the bridge, the thought came to me that I should give life one more chance. I decided I would walk across the bridge and see if someone on the other side would help me. Your office was the first place I saw, so I entered. If you had rejected me or been gruff, I think I would have turned around and jumped. But you were so kind and helpful, even though I had no money and I was a mess. Dr. Decker, you made the difference in my living or dying. Since you treated me, things have started to go my way, and now I feel that I truly want to live. And I will, thanks to you."

The man shook Dr. Decker's hand and walked out the door. Nelson sat back in his office chair, stunned. He was astonished to consider the effect of his shift in perception about the man. The doctor's willingness to join with this fellow and treat him had brought about a healing far beyond anything that Nelson had considered. It was a lesson that changed the doctor's career and his life.[10]

## A Miracle Is Never Lost

*A Course in Miracles* teaches that "A miracle is never lost. It may touch many people you have not even met, and produce undreamed-of changes in situations of which you are not even aware."

In my healing practice and ministry, I feel blessed to receive many letters and phone calls of appreciation for the positive changes that people have experienced through my books and workshops. It is awesome to me when I consider that these reports represent but a small portion of the healings and changes that actually occur.

As I look back on my own spiritual path and consider the many people who have touched and helped me in so many ways, I realize that I have acknowledged only a small percentage of them. Most of the people who have blessed me, sometimes even affected major transformations in my life, have not been aware of the miracles they induced.

A real healer must employ x-rays. Not photographic x-rays, but a kind of x-ray vision in which the healer looks at his or her practice through the eyes of Spirit. A true healer sees beyond the appearance of limited success and into the reality of great and dynamic healing.

We do not realize the depth, strength, and integrity of healing that we are actually offering. As teachers and healers (which all of us are, in one way or another) we are often distracted and even fooled by the appearance of the problems in our practice and the limitations we experience. But there is much more to reality than the limited scope of life that we perceive. Our capacity to give healing is total, and we give a lot more healing than we realize—especially in situations which seem challenging. In fact, the most difficult situations are the ones with the greatest potential for real transformation. *A Course in Miracles* also tells us, "The holiest place on earth is where an ancient hatred has become a present love." Remember this, and you will be unlimited in ability to heal.

## Truth or Appearances?

When my first book, *The Dragon Doesn't Live Here Anymore*, was published, I sent a copy to one of my favorite writers, Richard Bach, author of *Jonathan Livingston Seagull*.[11] One morning I went to my mailbox and found a handwritten postcard. The large letters were thoughtfully written:

> *Dear Alan,*
> *Thank you for your book and your warm words. It seems as though the family of those of us who do not believe in appearances is a large one!*
> > *Yours,*
> > *Richard Bach*

At any given moment in a healing practice (like all of life), we must choose between truth and appearance, between limitation and freedom, between fear and love. Your success as a healer, a mother, a business-person, or as the light of the world, depends entirely on the vision you choose to employ. You can see either perfection or problems; there is no in-between. Your ability to uplift and transform the lives of your children or your patients is entirely a function of your commitment to see strength where another sees only weakness. Your satisfaction and pride in everything you do depends on accepting your function as a vessel of blessing, no matter what the outer world seems to indicate. *The outer world has no power.* It is but a reflection of the inner world, a kingdom where you and God stand together as co-creators.

As Jonathan Livingston Seagull's teacher, Chiang, told him, *"The trick is to stop seeing yourself as trapped inside a limited body with a 42-inch wingspan...The trick is to know that your true nature lives, as perfect as an unwritten number, everywhere at once across space and time."*

The Chinese patriarch Chuang-Tsu taught the same principle thousands of years ago. He told, "In a dream I saw myself as a great butterfly with wings that spanned the entire universe. Now I am not quite sure if I am Chuang-Tsu dreaming I am a butterfly, or perhaps I am a butterfly dreaming I am Chuang-Tsu!"

You and I are all the most wonderful things we have imagined ourselves to be. We already have x-ray vision. Now it is up to us to use it. With x-ray vision we see ourselves as God sees us—wholly worthy, lovable, and vital to the unfoldment of Spirit's plan of perfection.

We need to remember the x-ray vision of the sage, Spinoza, who said, "To be who we truly are, and to become all that we are truly capable of becoming, is the only end in life." The world needs our x-ray vision. When we see with God, there is no end to the miracles we can create.

# WHERE CREDIT IS DUE

*It takes courage to remember God in places where Spirit is not usually acknowledged. When we follow the path with heart, we have the strength to do whatever we need to do.*

It seems that whenever I need to learn a lesson, the messenger finds me. Sometimes the next truth I need to know comes through a movie, a sunset, or the look in a friend's eyes. I am learning that I can never be separated from the path of my healing. Over and over again, I see that the CCCC (Cosmic Coincidence Control Center) is on the job.

One evening while flipping through the television channels I discovered a new kind of award show—*Best Comedy of the Year*. Similar to the Academy Awards for motion pictures, this event honored the best television, movie, and stand-up comedians. That evening I had some ironing to do, and the laughter from the tube seemed a perfect companion to pressing my shirts. After most of the trophies were presented, the emcee announced that the academy saw fit to honor one person who had made an outstanding lifetime contribution to the field of comedy in the media. The recipient was Norman Lear, the originator and producer of many of the funniest and most socially enlightening television comedy series of our time, including *All in the Family, The Jeffersons,* and *One Day at a Time*.

Norman rose and stepped spryly to the stage, enfolded by a standing ovation from his peers. In accepting the award he thanked many people associated with his success. Then he thanked someone else.

"I want to acknowledge another collaborator," Norman stated, "—the Spirit of God."

I put the iron aside.

"I must give credit to that still, small voice that speaks to me in the middle of the night," he went on. "I know this might sound a little sentimental, but I firmly believe that if we honored that Presence, the world would be in love and at peace."

He did it. He really did it. He had the guts to stand before that assembly and bear witness to the authorship of God. What a gift!

It takes courage to remember God in places where Spirit is not usually acknowledged. And that courage we have. When we follow the path with heart, we have the strength to do whatever we need to do.

This time on earth is not about leaving the earth and going to heaven; it is about bringing heaven to earth. Plenty of people have left the earth to go to heaven, and the earth is not much better for it. But how many of us have opened up the doors of our lives to let heaven be right here with us? In our jobs. In our relationships. In our sexuality. In our creativity. In our body. In everything, everywhere. Now.

The great visionary Teilhard de Chardin predicted:

*"Someday, after mastering the winds, the waves, and the tides,*
*we shall harness for God the power of love,*
*and then, for the second time in history,*
*man will have discovered fire."*

To succeed spiritually as well as materially, we need to give God a seat on the Board of Trustees. We can have seats, too, but unless God has a vote, nobody wins. As I read on a bumper sticker, "Unless Jesus is driving, you're just spinning your wheels." I would broaden this principle to say that when our guide is the Spirit of Love, only good can come of whatever we do.

The most successful people are those who are motivated not by fame or self-importance, but by love. Wally Amos, the creator of *Famous Amos* cookies, said, "The moment I stopped baking cookies to make money and started baking them to make people happy, my career took off and the amount of happiness in my life increased tremendously." Wally, like other successful creators, placed joy at the top of his list of priorities. Because he values love, he receives it in great measure. The miracle is that lovegivers usually receive what they seek in the world—and more. Not because they hunt for it, but because happiness is the natural result of service.

The principle of tithing applies not only to money, but to all of consciousness. We need to give Spirit at least 10% of our awareness, and credit Spirit as our most important advisor. This gives God a chance to get Her foot in the door of our life, and guide us in our worldly actions. We don't need to sit in a cave and meditate all day. That may be a true path for some; we have all probably done that in one life or another. Now, for most of us, it's about living in the world with our heart turned to Spirit. We receive the gifts of Spirit with one hand, and give to the world with the other. Like Norman Lear.

I don't know exactly how Norman's comments were received by the comedy academy. I do know that millions of people across the nation heard that Norman Lear considers God responsible for his success. And God considers Norman Lear responsible for His success.

# ROOM AT
# THE TOP

*The power of the mind is the key to all
success. We create our entire experience
with our thoughts, and in any given moment
we can change our life by seeing from
a higher perspective. If you know who
you are, you know what you deserve—the best—
and the world is at your fingertips.*

I dreamed I was competing in a beauty contest. In this competition, the entrants were judged on appearance, talent, and presentation. There were to be winners for music, dance, and other forms of creative self-expression.

As the judges announced the winners, I was disappointed to find that I was not among them. When the last prize had been given, I approached a judge and asked her why I had not won in any of the categories.

"Oh, you could have won!" she replied. She showed me the paper with the scoring on it. I saw that in many categories I had as many points as the winner.

"Then why didn't I win?" I asked.

"Because you didn't believe you would." She explained: "In this contest, your belief determines the results. Those who won expected that they would. They exuded joy and confidence as they offered themselves. The only difference between you and those who won was that somewhere in your mind and heart you didn't feel you deserved to win. That's why, even though you had as many points as the other participants, they received the prizes. Their belief in themselves and what they were doing was the element that drew us to vote for them. We had to—that's the way the law of winning works."

I was stunned. Disappointed, but excited. All I had to do was believe in myself.

Then came a P.S.: "Oh, yes—in this contest, everyone can win. Whoever believes in himself is sure to receive a prize. There are no limits to the number of winners."

What an amazing model for all of life! Belief in yourself is the key. That belief—or lack of it—makes all the difference in having, being, and expressing all that you truly want. If you know who you are, you know what you deserve—the best—and the world is at your fingertips.

*The power of the mind is the key to all success.* In any given moment we create our entire experience with our thoughts, and in any given moment we can change our life by seeing from a higher perspective.

## The Power of a Thought

Several years ago I was conducting a weekend retreat, and I discovered that I had forgotten my alarm clock. I needed to get up early the next morning to teach a class, so a friend offered to let me use his wristwatch with an alarm on it.

After enjoying a good night's sleep, I awakened to the beep of the alarm. I looked out the window and noticed that it was still dark outside on this winter morning. "Great!" I thought to myself, "I have some time to meditate." I felt refreshed and enthusiastic about rising and joining my mind with God's as I ventured into this new day. I went on to enjoy a precious time listening to the inner voice that guides me.

When my meditation was complete, I opened my eyes to discover that the sun had not yet risen. "What time is it, anyway?" I wondered. I looked at the watch. It was 3 o'clock in the morning. I had awakened not to the alarm, but to the watch's hourly beeper!

Now here is the fascinating twist in this metaphysical plot: My next thought was, "God, it's early...I've only gotten four hours' sleep...That's not very much at all." Then I began to feel tired. I wanted to go back to bed—but only after I knew the time! When I thought I had gotten seven hours' rest, I felt great. But the *thought*, "I should be tired," was enough to make me tired.

That morning's experience was a great lesson in the power of thoughts. It demonstrated to me that mind is indeed the source of our experience. Everything that comes to us is a result of the thoughts we plant in this garden universe. We think, and the God within us provides the energy for those thoughts to sprout into manifestation. We can do as we wish with that power. Such is the depth and magnitude of God's trust and belief in us, His Children.

### Matching God's Vision

To be truly happy, we need to match God's belief in us. In some fund-raising drives, generous donors offer "matching funds." They promise to donate $10,000 or $100,000 to the cause if the organization can raise an equal amount from individual members.

In a sense, God had provided us with the greatest matching fund in the universe. Spirit has given us unlimited love, fantastic talents and potentials, and an endless wealth of opportunities to manifest our good. We need to love and believe in ourselves enough to match God's vision of who we are. We accomplish this by seeing ourselves as whole, as God sees us.

The path to success is seen through unified vision. Through one eye God is constantly beholding perfection, and through the other eye we see our view. If both eyes are not seeing the same vision of wholeness, we stumble through life, unfocused and unclear about who we are. We wonder what we are doing here, where we are going, and what our purpose is. Such confusion is caused not by a haphazard universe; it is due to the fact that our eye is not seeing life from the same front-row seat as God's.

Because we believe we stumbled into the theatre of life by accident, we feel relegated to a remote seat in the balcony, from which we can't see much of the action on stage. We squint and squirm and we're not really sure what the play is about. Occasionally we get a glimpse of the story, and it does seem to be entertaining, but we sure wish we had a better idea of what's going on.

When we feel so distant from the heart of our life, we need but look in our own hand, where we will find a ticket for a valuable orchestra seat. From this place of clear vision we can enjoy the same play that God wouldn't miss for the world. When we see the play with singular vision, we discover that it is indeed a masterful one.

Now we can look upon ourselves and all the events in our life through the eyes of love. Our eye beholds the same beauty as God's, and we enjoy perfect spiritual vision. We are not sinners; we have just needed some practice with depth perception. We have been seeing mostly surface appearances, while God is always aware of the truth behind appearances. When we line up our focus with God's, immediately we see our right place and the next step on the path. That step is always related to belief in ourselves and trust in telling the truth. When we remember that we walk with Spirit, we know that we cannot lose.

There is room at the top for everyone. There is enough of everything we want and need in life. We can all be great and successful in what we most love to do. The universe is masterfully designed so that each of us can shine in our own field of talent. When our life doesn't seem to be working, it is not because we have a shortage of talents or opportunities; it is because we have not had the faith or courage to step forward and do what we would most love to do. Even the smallest step in the direction of sharing our talents is richly rewarded.

There is no limit to everyone having it all. As one sage taught, "God is a circle whose center is everywhere, and whose circumference is nowhere." Our next step is to withdraw our attention from the idea of boundaries and return it to the center of our creativity, where we were born to live. Poverty and failure do not befit the Children of God. We were born to live in abundant joy, and we do not need to settle for anything less. There is room at the top for everyone!

# ONE OF OUR BOYS MADE IT

*People often ask me if I have converted.
"No," I tell them, "I have expanded."*

I am often asked, "How can you be Jewish and profess such a love for Jesus and his teachings?"

I had occasion to reflect on my heritage and my relationship with Jesus when I was invited to address the annual conference of Unity ministers. Standing at the podium on the stage of the great auditorium at Unity Village in Missouri, I scanned the faces of 500 Christian clergymen and women. Here was a prestigious gathering of religious leaders! Although I had an address prepared, I put my papers aside and began with this statement:

"Now it might strike some of you as strange that a fellow named Cohen should stand here and address this august assembly of Christian ministers—but then again, word has it that one of my relatives is very popular around here."

There was a moment of pregnant silence, and then the audience broke into a rolling peal of laughter. Together we experienced a deep sense of joining in the part of ourselves that was far beyond labels or religious distinctions. There was no sense of separateness; we felt but a living awareness of our spiritual sameness, a reality that transcends names and forms.

Jesus was one who taught the universal presence of love rather than the limitation of labels. He was and is an example of a soul at peace with all of life. To confine Jesus to Christianity would be like limiting light to the sun. Light shines from many stars, and it brings illumination wherever there are no masks to block it. Jesus came not to build more walls around the heart, but to remove them.

## The Unity of Love

Years ago my spiritual teacher, Hilda, received a phone call from a Jewish television comedian seeking prayers for healing.

"Do you mind if I pray in the name of Jesus?" she asked him.

"Not at all," he responded, "—as long as you don't mind that he was Jewish."

To deny the Christ force in Judaism is to overlook the unity of love. We need to realize that Jesus was himself a Jew. He was born of Jewish parents, he was circumcised, he studied the Torah, he had a Bar Mitzvah, he ate kosher food, and when he taught his truth in the synagogues of Galilee and Jerusalem he was reverently called "Rabbi." After he was crucified, Jesus was entombed according to orthodox Jewish practices. There is no question that Jesus lived in the Jewish faith. For that reason those of us who are Jewish may find a rich pride in knowing that this great one arose from our midst.

Sooner or later every Jew needs to look upon Jesus through the eyes of peace. This does not mean that one must become a Christian, attend church, convert, or follow a dogma. It just means that we must honor his light. To deny his light is to refuse our own, to lock a chamber of healing from the altar of our heart. We can continue to wholeheartedly honor Moses and all of the Jewish prophets and traditions. Being true messengers of healing, these great ones would recognize their own light in Jesus and respectfully honor him as a loving brother. As we open our arms to enfold the truth that God is everywhere, we are healed.

### Whose Son?

There was a pious Jewish man in Israel whose eldest son went to America for a visit. After a year's absence, the father received a letter from the boy informing him that he had become a Christian.

The father became very upset at this news, and decided to go see a friend to seek help with his dilemma.

"Samuel," the father reticently began, "I just received a most disturbing letter from my son Avi...You won't believe this, but he has become a Christian!"

Samuel listened carefully, and paused for a moment of serious thought. Then he answered, "As a matter of fact, Ben, I would understand. I have never told anyone this, but since you have been so honest with me, I must tell you that I, too, had a son. Years ago he moved away to a far country and, like your boy, he became a Christian."

Both men sat in silence, trying to digest what they now knew. Ben and Samuel were surprised that they shared this predicament, and they wondered what to do. After grappling with the situation, the two men decided to go seek the advice of the rabbi.

"Rabbi, we both had sons who became Christians," the elders confided, "and we would like to know what you have to say about this."

The rabbi listened patiently, stroking his beard slowly and rhythmically as the two men spoke. Then the learned one responded.

"My dear friends," the sage addressed the men, "this is most astounding news! Your dilemma is significant to me because I, too, had a son. When he was a young man he left my home and he became a Christian. Quite frankly, this has troubled me for many years, and I must tell you that I have found no easy answer."

Startled at their mutual predicament, the men deliberated on what their recourse might be. Finally the rabbi suggested that, failing their own resources, they turn to God for help. Together they stepped to the altar and entered into silent prayer. After several minutes of silence the rabbi spoke for the group.

"Almighty God," the rabbi entreated, "all three of us had sons who became Christians, and we do not know what to do. What can you tell us?"

At that very moment a miraculous event occurred. A great beam of light shined down upon the altar. Instantly the men sensed that they were in the holy presence. Then they heard a deep and powerful voice speak from above: "I had a son..."

### True Conversion

People often ask me if I have converted. No, I tell them, I have expanded. I live in a win/win world, a holographic universe in which all the parts contain the whole and reflect it from every viewing point. I am definitely Jewish and I definitely love Jesus. I don't see any contradiction. Am I a Jew for Jesus? Yes. Am I a Boy for Buddha? Naturally. And I'm a Man for Moses, an Alan for Allah, and a Cohen for Confucius. If there's a party happening, I am for whoever is throwing it. I can empathize with the fellow who quit being an atheist because there weren't enough holidays. I celebrate all the holidays. To me the religions are like different types of lights—incandescent, fluorescent, mercury vapor—they all shine when you turn them on.

The kind of conversion we need now on the planet is not one of form or labels. What we need to convert is *our way of thinking*. We need to think bigger, broader, more in terms of living together in harmony. More wars have been fought and more people have been killed in the name of religion than for any other reason. I do not and cannot believe that God would take sides. God is on all sides, and none. The conversion that we so sorely need now is to lift our minds up to see how we can support one another in our remembrance of love, rather than attack our differences. It is not so important whether we call ourself Jew, Christian, or Muslim, but that we call ourself friend. Then and only then shall we see God walk on earth again.

## The Religion of the Heart

I do not believe that Jesus sought to establish a religion separate or in competition with others. If Jesus walked today I wonder how he would feel about the separations that have been created in his name. So many of us have used the name of Jesus and the Christian religion to justify actions that have little to do with the great healing principles Jesus came to glorify. Carl Jung said, "Thank God I am not a Jungian!" I wonder if Jesus would thank God that he is not a Christian.

Jesus is happy to work within the Christian religion, without the Christian religion, and within or without any other religion. Spirit welcomes all opportunities to extend forgiveness. The religion of love is not confined to a rectangle of stone walls; the creed of sharing is where you are. To find the Christ in your own heart is to become all that Jesus was and is. The God who lived and lives within him is willing to work just as powerfully within you and me. Jesus said, "Even greater things than I, shall you do." This promise applies to everyone, no matter what religion through which we come to the light. The word "Christ" means "the anointed one." If you find the light, you are anointed, and you are one with the Christ. Now we, too, must claim our perfection.

## Where the Church Is

The churches we attend externally are reflections or representations of the inner church, where the flame of love burns eternally on the altar of the heart. The church that Jesus referred to was not simply the one to which we claim membership or visit on the sabbath morning. It is a presence that we carry with us wherever we go, a sanctuary of inner comfort in which we may find refuge when the struggle of separation has become more than we can bear. As a sage explained, "Within each of us there is a church service going on all the time; it is up to us to enter it."

Jesus brought the world a demonstration of one to whom the peace of God was more important than anything the world had to offer. His interest was in healing, not in a personal institution. He had no dogma, only compassion. He prescribed no practices, save forgiveness. He was not concerned with differences between people; he saw all as innocent. He exacted no penance or punishment; his joy was the awakening of those he touched. He was not a slave to fear, but a master of love. He may aptly be called the Christ, the savior, for that is what he saw and found in everyone.

## The Time of Joining

We must use our religions and our nations to join, and not separate. Swami Satchidananda's Yogaville community in Virginia has built a beautiful shrine in the form of a great lotus flower. In the shrine there stands an altar to each of the world's religions. On each altar rests a symbolic holy book of that faith, etched with a passage from that religion stating that there is one God, and that God is the light of the world. At the center of the circular temple a laser beam emits rays of pure light to the altars at the outer wall, like a great illuminated wheel. What a magnificent metaphor for the truth that God is one energy, shining healing into the world through many rays, reflected on many altars, yet born of one Perfect Source.

Now there are more and more ecumenical gatherings of teachers of God. Ministers, priests, rabbis, swamis, monks, Native American medicine men and women, and a colorful array of spiritual leaders are coming together to celebrate our oneness. Catholic convents are offering Zen meditation retreats, Hindu shrines honor Jesus on their altar, and Amazon tribal healers are showing up at psychic conferences in Pennsylvania. A few years ago Dr. Jerry Jampolsky, author of the popular *Love is Letting Go of Fear*, brought the King of the Zulus to the Human Unity Conference in Boston! Our world is getting smaller, and that is a great blessing: the more we can see each other, the more we can see that we are the same.

One of the pleasures I enjoy about browsing in spiritual bookstores is that I can find on the same shelf books on Buddhist Dharma, Jewish Kabbalah, and Hawaiian Huna healing—all roads of awakening that lead us to the same mountaintop. Our Age of Communication is bringing us a great blessing, and that is joining; the realization that the way to God is to become like God—embracing the unity in our diversity.

### *How Far You Can Go*

Perhaps our unity is most clearly demonstrated in a conversation overheard at a recent ecumenical clergy convention. Father Quinn and Rabbi Goldstein were relaxing in the lounge, getting to know one another through some casual after-dinner conversation.

"Tell me, Father," the rabbi inquired, "Is there an opportunity for advancement in your profession?"

"Well," the priest explained, "we do have a local diocese over which a Bishop presides. Rumor has it that he will be leaving soon, and it is possible that I could become the Bishop of the region."

"I see," the rabbi responded. "What about after that?"

"As you may know, Rabbi Goldstein, there is also the honored office of Cardinal. Mind you, now, I am not an ambitious man—but if the Lord called me to serve in such a position, I would pray to be worthy of it."

"That's very nice," Rabbi Goldstein answered. "Could you go any higher?"

"Now, rabbi, you are asking about a very improbable situation. The only Christian leader higher than a Cardinal is the Pope himself. When our Heavenly Father calls the Pope to his reward, the College of Cardinals holds a sacred meeting. At this gathering the clergymen listen for divine inspiration to elect God's choice for the new Pope. If by some great plan of destiny the Lord guided the Cardinals to choose me, there is a very slight chance that I might one day be the Pope."

"And what could you become beyond the Pope?"

"Heavens, man!" the priest stood up and exclaimed, "What do you expect me to become—Jesus Christ?"

"Why not?" the rabbi smugly answered, "—One of our boys made it!"

# Section Four

# *The Path with Heart*

# THE CITY
# OF REFUGE

*There is a safe place within each of us:*
*a state of consciousness, an awareness of*
*the innocence in which we are forgiven*
*and freed of any sense of sin or separation.*
*God has never punished anyone; it is we*
*who hurt ourselves by laboring under a*
*concept that we are sinful creatures*
*rather than Children of the Most High.*

On the Big Island of Hawaii there is an amazing place called "The City of Refuge." In the ancient Hawaiian tradition, if a person committed a crime, they would be forgiven if they could get to the City of Refuge before their accuser—usually the royalty—could catch them.

The City of Refuge is located at a bay several miles south of the former king's city of Kona on the western shores of the island of Hawaii. The place exudes an ancient mystical vibration, echoing the chants of a people who saw God in that land. The aqua surf pounds a rhythm against its black lava rock shores just as it did in the days when King Kamehameha walked the Kona coast.

When the criminal reached the City of Refuge (usually by swim-ming across the bay), he found the ancient *kahunas* (priests) waiting for him. Quickly the *kahunas* prayed and performed an ablution ceremony, and within hours the condemned person was freed to return to society and carry on as if no crime had ever been committed.

As I walked among the ancient buildings of the City of Refuge, I considered the spiritual symbolism of the site. The Hawaiian religion is founded on an important process called "*ho'oponopono,*" which most easily translates as "forgiveness." I have participated in *ho'oponopono* workshops and discovered that the principles are identical to *A Course in Miracles*, the teachings of Jesus, the basic tenets of Buddha, and the spiritual vision of Native American healing: All is alive; everything we see contains the spirit of the Living God; and to be happy we need to release our judgments and give love where we once felt separated.

The City of Refuge offered me a more subtle lesson. I gained a deeper understanding that opened my eyes and allowed me to see a powerful truth about forgiveness: The City of Refuge is *within* me.

There is a safe place within each of us: a state of consciousness, an awareness of the innocence in which we are forgiven and freed of any sense of sin or separation. Jesus called it the Kingdom of Heaven. He told us in many ways that the Kingdom is already a part—and the whole—of who we truly are. When we feel that we have sinned, we must flee to the City of Refuge. Remember that the ancient Hawaiian had to run or swim to the City of Refuge before his accuser could catch him. So, too, do we need to immediately get to our center of forgiveness when we believe we deserve punishment.

Our accusers are not people. They are our own attack thoughts, our judgments about ourself, our sense of being liable for punishment by God. The moment we believe we have offended God, we must quickly take refuge. That sanctuary is not found in a place, but in the remembrance that God is far beyond our concept of offense and retaliation. God has never punished anyone. God only loves and forgives. It is we who hurt ourselves by laboring under a concept that we are sinful creatures rather than Children of the Most High. Once we are established in the truth of a God that is consistently and unchangeably forgiving, we are released. Then we are free to get on with our life in the creative and positive way we were intended to live.

The ego is the devil's fisherman; it is well-versed in ways to catch us in a net of thoughts of sin and punishment. If we do not forgive ourselves quickly, our sense of guilt begins to spin a web that binds our mind and prevents us from seeing the truth of our innocence and the guiltlessness of those who love us. Be careful not to listen to the voice of fear, or you will soon find your heart in a cold and barren prison, and you will wonder why God has deserted you. But it is not God who has deserted you; it is the thoughts of isolation that bar your vision from the light that enfolds you always. Loneliness is the result of the thought that we are outside of the love that created us. And we are not.

*A Course in Miracles* tells us that we are too tolerant of our mind wandering, and there are no such things as idle thoughts. "What gives rise to an entire world," the course teaches, "could hardly be called idle."

## Peace Now, As I Choose It

Riding home on the plane from the Big Island, I began to criticize myself for not living up to my expectations while visiting a friend there. My self-criticism spawned a wave of guilt, and soon I found myself at the end of a spear of accusation. The spearholder called his fellow tribesmen, and before long I was anticipating going through hours of metaphysical Indiana Jones tactics before I would be able to escape the warriors of dark thinking.

Then it occurred to me: *The City of Refuge.* If I could just make it to the City of Refuge before my accusers (my attack thoughts) arrested me, I could be free. I imagined running quickly to the *kahunas*, knowing for sure that their forgiveness could save me.

I took a deep breath. "I can have peace now if I choose it," I reminded myself. I looked out the window of the plane. It was dark, and yet I could feel the light within the darkness. I breathed again. I closed my eyes and imagined telling a beloved angel what had happened. I looked into her eyes and felt great compassion and understanding. It was only my own condemnation that injured me. I saw her as she saw me, and my fears left me. I felt loved and forgiven. I was free. I had reached the City of Refuge.

# THE
# PRESENT

*To grow, you must be willing
to let your present and future
be totally unlike your past.
Your history is not your destiny.*

Recently a couple came to me for counseling to help them overcome a roadblock in their relationship. They had been together for a short time, and they wanted to create a meaningful and lasting relationship. Both of them had been through numerous relationships in the past, and together they were seeking to develop a new and more rewarding pattern.

Each partner began by offering a lengthy history of the errors and painful patterns he or she had created in their past relationships. I heard them justifying the problems they were having now by using their past mistakes as evidence for their limitations; it was as if they were acting as lawyers for their own prosecution. I felt that we were getting nowhere.

"Let's stop here for a moment," I suggested. "Both of you have told me a lot about what happened to you months and years ago. But what is happening for you now?"

Both of them were a little startled. They thought for a moment, and the man responded first. He faced his partner, took her hands, looked her in the eyes, and told her, "Ellen, I care about you a lot. You mean a great deal to me, and I really want to be with you."

I turned to look at Ellen. Tears were rolling down her cheeks. "Marty," she responded, "I feel the same way about you. Sometimes I get scared, and when I feel afraid, I retreat into my old patterns of protection. But that's not what I really want to do. I want to keep my heart open to you and offer you all that I am."

We all felt the power of the truth in that moment. Each of us lit up as we sensed the healing energy that was flowing from their hearts to each other. The cloud of confusion lifted as the couple began to see themselves more clearly and tell the truth about what they were feeling. Marty and Ellen acknowledged that they loved and wanted to be with one another more than anyone or anything else. Their fears, reservations, and mistrust, we discovered together, were based not on their true feelings about one another, but on their histories and perceptions of those with whom they had walked in the past. As they came into the freedom of *now*, they were released from the constriction of *then*.

When we use our past as a guide to the present, we disempower ourselves. As Richard Bach tells us, "Argue for your limitations, and sure enough they're yours." If you feel plagued by a pattern of unsuccessful relationships, health challenges, or business disappointments, there is one sure way to change your pattern:

*Release the past and begin to create what you want now.*

Your vision of what you truly want must be stronger and more real to you than your thoughts about what you have previously created. Your past errors were due only to unconsciousness, or a blind spot in the field of your awareness. The way to get rid of a blind spot is to expand your vision. If you see more now than you did then, you will not repeat your errors, and a new and more positive, constructive pattern is sure to ensue.

### *Tigers or Strawberries?*

There is a story about a man who was being chased through the forest by two hungry tigers. He ran to the edge of a cliff, and seeing no other means of escape but a hanging vine, he began to shimmy down it. As he came to the end of the vine, the man looked down and saw below him two more hungry tigers waiting for him there. An unenviable predicament, indeed!

So what did our friend do? He looked around and saw that there were some wild strawberries growing out of the side of the cliff. Smiling, he reached out, plucked a few berries, and ate them—and they were the sweetest strawberries he ever tasted!

Tigers behind us, tigers ahead of us, strawberries within our reach. A perfect metaphor for living consciously, being open to the gifts available to us now. Enjoying the gifts of the moment, and trusting God. There are always tigers out there, and there are always strawberries. Which do we choose? We can have whatever we pay attention to, and we will receive more of whatever we focus on. It is a dynamic law of living.

It takes courage, wisdom, and trust to live in the moment. To grow, you must be willing to have your present and future be totally unlike your past. Are you willing to go beyond your past errors? Our history is not our destiny. When we open to new possibilities, we join our mind with God's. God sees only what is happening now, and that is always wonderful, creative, and empowering. *Now* is the door to the healing power of heaven.

With the release of the past goes all of our sins, errors, and losses.

They remain with us only as we choose to carry them along our journey—and they are heavy luggage indeed!

## *How Long?*

The Zen Buddhists have a splendid parable about releasing the past. Two monks were walking through the woods when they came upon a woman standing at the bank of a shallow river.

"Could you please help me cross this river?" she asked.

"Certainly," answered one of the monks. He politely lifted her up and carried her to the other side. She thanked him, and the monks and the woman went their respective ways.

Several hours later, the monk who had carried the woman noticed that his friend seemed disturbed. "Is there something on your mind, my brother?" he asked.

"Yes, there is," his companion answered. "You know it is against the rules of our order to touch a woman, much less carry her in your arms!"

"I know," the first monk answered, "...but I put her down several hours ago."

What past limitations are you carrying with you? Are you using the past against yourself, justifying your littleness though you were born to be great? Are you re-creating your past by focusing on your problems rather than your possibilities?

There is only one useful attitude about the past, and that is *gratefulness*. When we bless our history, it becomes our friend. God's vision sees *all things as good*, including the experiences that have made us stronger, more aware, and closer to the love that we are here to cultivate. When we see with the vision of the heart, we realize that we have received nothing but love, for love is what we are.

To be healed and successful in our relationships, our work, and our spiritual growth, we must be perfectly honest with ourselves. We must acknowledge where our life is, and where we want to go. To truly move ahead, we must cast to the wind the cocoons of the past, for we cannot live in an old shell and fly at the same time. Butterflies need room to spread their wings. You have the power to let go of everything that has ever stood between you and your dreams. Now your life is new, and you are the one who can let it be magnificent. Give yourself the present.

# THE
# COUNSELOR

*The way out of the rat race is not to
become more aggressive in it,
but to invite the vision of
One who sees beyond it.*

One Saturday night I tuned in to an episode of the new *Star Trek* television series. To my delight, I found that the original series has been reincarnated with the touch of the mystic that has made those fabled voyages so dear to the hearts of metaphysicians.

I was especially pleased to discover the addition of a new crew member to the bridge of the *Enterprise*—a psychic guide. Called "the counselor," this woman has a very specific role: to offer the captain advice on matters that go beyond the scope of their scientific instruments.

In this episode, the crew of the *Enterprise* was accosted by the leaders of several planets, each of whom claimed the right to custody of an intergalactic hitchhiker whom the *Enterprise* had taken aboard. The captain of the *Enterprise* struggled with the demands of the leaders. In his attempts to discern the truth of their statements, he found himself in a quandary about his rightful role in responding. After grappling with the leaders for a while, the captain became frustrated with their petitions. Then he turned to the resident psychic. "Counselor?" he appealed.

The counselor was still for a moment. Then, upon feeling the dynamics of the situation, she advised the captain that each of these men was telling the truth as far as they knew it, but their perceptions and demands were clouded by anger.

Considering this advice, the captain invited the leaders aboard the *Enterprise*. A heated debate ensued, which led to one man revealing that he was in love with the woman who named the hitchhiker as the father of her unborn child.

"Now the real truth is starting to come!" the counselor interjected. Then all the parties began to reveal the deeper feelings which were fueling their arguments. Finally the couple who truly loved one another got together, everyone went home happy, and the *Enterprise* shot off the screen to another adventure.

Pondering on the episode, I was thrilled by the symbolism of the psychic on the *Enterprise*. To me, the crew on the bridge of that mythical vessel has always represented the different parts of our mind and how they interact to create the events in our life. We have the Science Officer, Mr. Spock, whose god is logic; for him, reason is the path to truth. Then there is the voice of emotion, portrayed by Dr. McCoy, who is moved primarily by intense feelings. The captain of the vessel, Kirk, takes all the information given to him by these critical officers, and makes decisions about which direction the ship is to go.

The addition of the intuitive counselor to the bridge of the new *Enterprise* is the acknowledgment of the voice of higher knowing. Our mind and our feelings give us some information—sometimes correct, but often deceptive—about our world. If we depend on thinking and feeling alone to make our decisions for us, we find ourselves in a tailspin of confusion. When those faculties do not satisfy our need to know the truth, we must turn to a higher voice for real guidance. The way out of the rat race is not to become more aggressive in it, but to invite the vision of One who sees beyond it.

### *The Voice That Knows*

One of the ways that I know God is through observing the presence of intuitive guidance in living creatures. Living in Maui, I have the delight of seeing the great Blue Humpback whales return to these waters every winter. Each year around Thanksgiving, these huge mammals of the sea come to the islands to mate, bear their young, and enjoy the warm Pacific waters.

The aspect of the humpbacks' odyssey that most amazes me is that they return to *exactly* the same spot each year. There is a seven-mile strait between the islands of Maui and Lanai, and it is to this particular nesting zone that the whales swim every winter.

In the spring, the humpbacks set off northward and return to their summer home in the waters off the coast of Canada and Alaska. Then, come next December, the swimming giants find their way through 5,000 *miles* of deep blue sea to the *precise* pinpoint of a breeding zone. What a fantastic navigation system!

Now here is something that I find even more astounding: It is not just the humpback species that returns to the same place, but *exactly the same whales!* Whale researchers have developed a system of identifying individual whales, whose flukes are as unique as our fingerprints. The scientists have charted the whales that show up every winter, and they are the same whales that were here the previous year. How wondrous is the intelligence that guides them!

There is a voice within the humpbacks that knows how to help them find their mates, successfully bear their young, and enjoy a winter of play in warm waters. Wouldn't it be marvelous if we could do the same?

We can. (It only took me 35 years to learn to go to a warm place for the winter!) The same wondrous wisdom that directs the humpbacks is available to guide us. If we are open to listening, we will hear the direction in which we need to go to find and express our good.

It is the voice within the heart that speaks gently, with the conviction of One who truly knows. This voice does not speak of judgment, attack, or fear, but with the clearest and most compassionate understanding. It is the voice of peace, calling to us through our heart, always available to help us with our current need. There is no issue too large or small for the voice to handle. It is the voice of God, willing to serve us wherever we are on our path of awakening. The inner counselor offers the gentlest yet most powerful wisdom.

When we seek help, we need but turn within. Emerson said, "We may search the entire world for happiness, but unless we carry it with us, we will find it not." Like the fabled musk deer who roams the mountains and valleys to find the source of an enchanting fragrance, only to discover that the aroma is emanating from itself, we carry our own answers within us. The journey ends where it began.

# BORN TO LOVE

*A being can become so alienated from his source that, when put in the presence of what would make him truly happy, he is afraid. All the love that we are seeking is already here.*

*The author and The Yogi*

February is traditionally the month in which we honor lovers. The month, warmed by the glow of Valentine's day, is an especially wonderful reminder of the truth of love, for everyone is included in the celebration of lovers. May is for Mom, June is for Dad, and Christmas is for Jesus. But in February, *everyone* can get into the act! Indeed we are *all* lovers.

Considering how we were born to love, I find it painful to consider that we often block ourselves from feeling that holy feeling we were created to enjoy. True love comes to us every moment of every day, from every possible angle. It is up to us whether and when we will accept it into our heart.

Perhaps the hardest thing to believe about the way we hurt ourselves is that we are afraid of love. It seems incredible that we fear the thing that we desire most. We deny our good to an alarming degree.

I learned this surprising lesson one day when I took my baby parrot, Yogi, outside to play. The previous night I had been reading the parrot manual, which explained that parrots love to play in trees. This seemed like a downright natural idea. So there we were the next morning, Yogi and me, facing the limbs of a tree in the backyard.

I lifted Yogi up to a branch and nudged him to get onto it. To my surprise, he scurried back up my arm to my shoulder, where he felt safe. I offered him the tree again, and once more he retreated to his familiar zone.

So I had a little talk with Yogi. I held the feathered guy up to my eye level and told him, "You are a bird." (This can be a difficult concept to get across to a pet who believes he is human.) I pointed: "This is a tree." Yogi tilted his head and looked at me quizzically. My lecture continued. "Birds live in trees," I explained. "Birds like trees. Most of your ancestors lived in a tree just like this one. Why don't you try it? You might even like it! If not for me, at least do it for your family."

Yogi lifted his head and blurted out, "I love you!" (He says that when he is afraid—perhaps he is more human than I thought!) Then he looked at me with one of his questioning looks, as if to say, "What are you talking about?"

I tried to get him to step onto the branch a few more times, but eventually it became clear to me that even though this was his natural habitat, Yogi did not feel safe in the tree. One more time he withdrew from the branch and scampered onto my shoulder. I decided to give up on the idea, and Yogi and I started back toward the house.

Then it dawned on me: It is possible for a being to become so alienated from his source that, when put in the presence of what would make him truly happy, he is afraid. More specifically, we human beings have learned to be so separate from our source—which is love—that when faced with the very presence that could heal us, we turn away. We run to what we believe is our safety zone. We escape into alcohol, drugs, work, our mind, sex, and a mire of relationships that seem to be striving for love but are actually a litany against it. We create a million ways of armoring ourselves from the joy that we really seek. We believe we are making ourselves safe, but we are actually deadening our hearts to the life we were born to enjoy. A parrot afraid of a tree. A person afraid of love. It was an all-too-painful, yet liberating metaphor.

Kabir said, "I laugh when I hear that the fish in the water is thirsty." We live in a world where billions of people are screaming for love. What, I wonder, if all the love that we are seeking is here and available already? What if most of the activities, the business, the *busy-ness* of the world is our way of shielding ourself from the love which, if we would only let our guard down for a moment, would heal us instantly?

I looked back over my shoulder at the tree which Yogi rejected. It offered a parrot's playground of many branches with just the kinds of knots and gnarls and twists that he loves to walk and munch on in his cage. I knew that if he ever really let himself play on the tree, he would have a field day. It was only his fear that stood between him and his delight.

Then I thought of all the opportunities I have had to love, but which I rejected out of fear. I remembered people who have genuinely loved me, and I ascribed ulterior motives to their actions. People who wanted to hug me, and I pulled away because I feared that they wanted something from me. Friends who have been there for me when I needed them the most, but I felt I had to do it all myself. A God who has always been ready and willing to heal me, but whom I have denied because I was not ready or willing to receive my good. Not very different from the bird afraid of a tree.

And yet all of it comes as a lesson. All of our experiences are experiments in this school of awakening in which we are enrolled. The wonderful gift about this school is that we always have another opportunity to do what we do with more love and awareness. I am free to choose again, and so are you.

Since that morning at the tree with Yogi, I have been more open to receive the love that is offered to me. It has been a new beginning for me. I appreciate my friends and the world more than ever. When I wake up I see the sun as a gift—and the rain, as well. I remember a piece of advice from Kahlil Gibran: *Awake at dawn and give thanks for another day of loving.*

This morning I took Yogi out to the tree again. This time I very gently offered him a lower branch. Easily he walked out onto it, and after a few moments he began to enjoy it. I was delighted. I loved and supported Yogi when he was afraid, and I rejoiced with him when he was ready to accept the kingdom for which he was born. Now I appreciate him even more for his gift of a precious lesson to me. Together, we're learning to step higher and fly.

*Yogi in his natural home*

# TRUE
# VALENTINES

*I made a vow to God that I would never
again delay expressing appreciation.
I cannot afford to wait to give love.*

I have discovered one of the greatest gifts of modern mass media. It is the Valentine's Day supplement in the local newspaper. As I opened this tabloid I was touched, tickled, and inspired to find hundreds of people publicly professing their love to their sweethearts, families, and friends.

I was delighted to find two entire pages of love notes and poems, from the sublime to the sappy to the outrageous:

> *Dooder, you're the biggest sweetheart in the world. I love you more than anything. See you at the altar in June. Love, Pooh Bear.*

> *Brad, my life is like a jigsaw puzzle and you're the special piece that makes the picture complete. Love, Mare.*

> *Terri, Dupa Dupa Dupa Dupa Dupa Dupa Dupa Dupa Dupa Dupa Dupa Dupa—that means Happy Valentine's Day. Love, Tom Dupa Dupa.*

These romantic writers expressed their hearts in a way that was real and alive for them. They were willing to declare their love and make it visible for all to look upon and feel. And in so doing they gave a great gift to everyone who read their poetry.

I began to ponder what it would be like if I expressed my love at that level of power and integrity *all the time*. What if you and I offered a bouquet of loving words to everyone we felt even a glimmer of appreciation for?

## *Don't Postpone Love*

I experienced an important demonstration of the power of expressing acknowledgement. On the final evening of our one-year intensive *Course in Miracles* study community, all the participants gathered together to share our appreciation for each other and our time together.

About 25 of us went out to a gazebo by the river, and sat in a candlelit circle. One at a time, each person sat in the center of the circle, and the rest of us told her or him what we most appreciated about them. Freely, without reservation, we described the gifts we had gained from being with them.

The process was amazing! A surprising number of unspoken appreciations were proclaimed, revealing many, many acts of thoughtfulness and caring that had been noticed throughout the year, but which were not acknowledged until that night. Before long, waterfalls of joyful tears were flowing. One fellow literally kissed the feet of his dearest friend. After about three hours we had completed sharing with only four people. The feeling, the vibration of that gathering was awesome.

When I told one woman how much I appreciated being in the community with her, she was surprised. "I thought you didn't like me," she told me.

"I really do treasure your friendship."

"How long have you felt that way?"

"Since October."

"It's August now—I wish I had known since October."

"I thought you knew."

"I guess I needed to hear it."

And I needed to tell it.

From that important evening I learned two major life lessons. First:

*All there is, is love.*

No matter what hassles and challenges each of us had gone through, when all the dust had settled, the reality was that we all loved one another very much.

The second principle is a natural extension of the first:

*We cannot afford to wait until the last moment to express our love.*

That night I made a vow to the God within me that I would never again delay expressing appreciation. I would not pass by opportunities to acknowledge my love or speak what is in my heart. What I learned that night affected a major change in my relationships; now they are so much more precious to me. As *A Course in Miracles* teaches, *"Love is the way I walk in gratitude."*

## *The First Valentine*

Do you know the origin of St. Valentine's Day? Like many holidays that we have grown accustomed to, the origin of Valentine's Day is deeply rooted in spiritual meaning. There is a touching legend that has brought me a new appreciation for this special day:

In the early years after Jesus walked the earth, all Roman citizens were ordered to bow down before the Roman gods. One Roman, Valentinus, felt his heart with Christ and Christ alone, and so he publicly refused to follow the edict. Impatient with infidels, the Roman governor had Valentinus thrown in jail and sentenced to death.

While in prison, Valentinus became friends with a jailer who had a daughter, a little blind girl named Julia. The jailer soon realized that Valentinus was a man of powerful faith and deep wisdom, so he brought young Julia to Valentinus each day for personal instruction.

Valentinus and Julia became dear friends. As the days passed, they grew devoted to one another—they shared learning, laughter, and the joys that only a friendship of the heart can bring.

Not long before Valentinus was scheduled to be executed, Julia came to him for help. "Valentinus, will I ever be able to see?" she asked.

"My dear child," the elder counseled, "God can do anything. Simply open your heart to love, and miracles will happen."

"Oh, yes, Valentinus," Julia responded, "I do trust that God can heal me!"

At that moment a great light flooded the prison cell. A luminous wave flowed over Valentinus and Julia like a brilliant mantle of peace. Both of them were touched and changed.

When the light had dissipated, Julia exclaimed, "My God, Valentinus, I can see! It is a miracle!"

"Praise be to God!" Valentinus proclaimed. Julia rested her head in his bosom and the two of them wept tears of joy.

The next time Julia came to visit Valentinus, he was gone. He had been taken to his execution. But there, lying on the prison bed, was a note for Julia written by Valentinus.

*Julia, now you know the power of God. Love God with all of your heart and you will be at peace. Trust in life. Trust love. Trust in the Heart that brought us together. I have been greatly blessed by*

*your beautiful spirit. Always remember that I love you and that
my love goes with you wherever you are.*

The letter was signed, *"Your Valentine."*

On the next day, February 14, Valentinus was executed in the adjoining courtyard. The almond tree in the courtyard bore flowers throughout the entire year that followed, as it does to this day. So it stands and still offers blessings, a symbol of the undying love that created miracles in the lives of Valentinus, Julia, and in our lives as well.

# MAJOR LEAGUE LOVERS

*You have a purpose. There is something
that you believe in, a vision that
stimulates you, a function that makes
your heart content as you fill it.
You are sure to achieve the goal
your heart truly values.*

God speaks to me through baseball movies. Perhaps this was not the method through which the Holy Spirit reached Elijah and the prophets, but I believe that may be simply because they did not play baseball during the biblical season. Given the opportunity, Jeremiah could have easily played for the Angels, and Ezekiel would probably have been an Astros fan.

Recently I saw a wonderful movie. *Major League* was billed as "a comedy with bats and balls." I found it to be a spiritual lesson about men with hearts. Picture a professional baseball team whose owner doesn't want it to win. Because she has a secret plan to move the Indian franchise to Miami, the team owner plots to create a huge loss to justify the move. So she hires a bunch of flunkies, weirdos, and losers, in hopes that they will take the team on an irreparable plunge to the league cellar.

And a wild bunch they are. This year's Indians are a funky crew indeed, including a punk rocker just out of jail, a voodoo enthusiast who converts his locker into a Haitian shrine, and an old-timer whose interest in interior decorating has surpassed his desire to win baseball games.

True to the owner's expectations, the Indians get off to a notoriously embarrassing start. After just a few games, the team's staunchest supporters are laughing at them, and the array of fans in the grandstands resembles a pattern of sesame seeds on a bagel—not much to speak of at all.

To make matters worse, every time the team wins, the owner makes the ballplayers' lives harder. She takes away their jet plane and replaces it with a funky old bus, decreases their salaries, and shuts off the hot water in the showers. When confronted, she pleads poverty due to the Indians' losing streak.

The poverty, of course, is not in reality—it is in her consciousness. It is hard to believe that the leader of a team would sabotage her own best interests. Yet, symbolically speaking, it is not at all unusual. There is a part of our mind that does not want us to win. More specifically, this mental antagonist believes that we will win by losing. This voice is called "the ego" by some, "the devil" by others. It is the element of our mind that is ruled by fear. This anxious dictator has a vested interest in staying in control. Its thirst for power is so vehement, in fact, that it will do *everything it can* to keep us from moving ahead and changing— even for the better. It is the debilitated guardian of the status quo.

Unchecked, the voice of fear rules our life and continually sabotages our happiness.

How, then, can we overcome this internal agent for our defeat?

I'll tell you how the Indians did it. They made the saboteur work for them. They took their frustrated energy and channeled it constructively. The Indians got together and decided that the only way to beat the self-defeating boss was to win ball games. They realized that if they continued to play flunky baseball, they would play right into her plot and they would all be fired at the end of the season. So there was no way out but to win.

The shared desire to succeed brought the team together. You should have seen these fellows play ball! The Indians rolled over the Rangers, swept the A's, and cooled the Red Sox' heels. They became unstoppable.

Finally the entire season came down to one playoff game with the Indians' most formidable adversaries, the Yankees. The Indians were stoked, but there was one fly in the ointment. The night before the game, the pitcher had slept with an attractive woman he had met in a bar. What he didn't know was that she was the wife of the shortstop. The wife, on a campaign to disempower her husband, told him about her affair just a few minutes before game time—not exactly the kind of move that would ensure harmony or success on the field!

The game came down to a tie in the ninth inning, and the ace pitcher was called in to put out the Yankee fire. Here we have a nervous pitcher needing to be strong, yet horribly embarrassed in the presence of the angry shortstop. As the pitcher steps onto the mound, the shortstop comes to confront him. The rest of the team, knowing what's happening, shudders. Behold a prime chemistry for the ruination of their pennant. The tension in the entire ballpark is thick.

The shortstop comes nose to nose with the pitcher and tells him point blank: "Let's cut through the nonsense; I have just one thing to say to you..." A long, tense silence ensues. *"Strike this joker out!"*

A great sigh of relief washes over the team. The shortstop has let the shared purpose of winning be bigger than his personal interest. The success of the team is more important to him than being right or holding a grudge. He is willing to be a winner.

The pitcher takes a deep breath; he looks as if a hundred-pound weight has been lifted off his shoulders. There's nothing to stop him now. He has the support of his team. The crowd is on its feet, calling for victory. He is ready.

He turns to face the batter, winds up, and throws a strike that the batter couldn't possibly touch. *Smokin'.* Then an even more intimidating strike two. *The kid is unbeatable.* Then the final pitch. *No holding back, now.* No resistance, no fear. Batter swings—strike three—he's out of there! The catcher is almost knocked over. The power of team spirit.

I loved the lessons of this movie. For one, the Holy Spirit can take anything you give it and turn it into a winner. This team of bumble-alongs had no class whatsoever—until they joined for a common purpose. Given the welcome for a miracle, Spirit took over, and winning was not only possible—it was quickly made real.

There is nothing that is beyond healing. No situation, no physical limitation, no relationship, no pattern of losing, no mental or emotional stuckness is beyond God's ability to transform it into a blessing. There is no dilemma that is too messy for God to clear up. Just ask God for help, and watch the tide turn.

Also, there are no bad guys. While the team owner seemed to be against the ballplayers, she actually turned out to serve them in the most powerful way. Without her challenging actions, the men would have had no motivation and finished the season in the cellar. Unwittingly she forced the ballplayers to work harder to thwart her sabotage and keep their jobs. When the men joined in this goal, their talents and abilities were quickly brought to action, drawing forth potentials they might never have developed otherwise. While the owner intended to make them losers, she ultimately gave them the perfect opportunity to become winners.

I am reminded of the biblical story of Joseph, whose brothers threw him into a pit to die, and later discovered he had been rescued and appointed assistant to Pharaoh in Egypt. When they "accidentally" met him and asked his forgiveness, he told them, "You meant it for evil, but God meant it for good." Seen in this light, our most difficult experiences become our best friends.

The shortstop's decision to forgive the pitcher was another powerful teaching. He had a choice: to carry on his personal vendetta, or go beyond it for the greater goal of the team's victory. How often you and I have the same choice—to clutch onto feeling like a victim, or let go to become a winner. We can't be both. We have to be powerful. There is no other way home.

And finally, there was the pitcher's strikeout. As he reared back to fire the final strike, I felt his intensity, his focus, his commitment. There was no other thought in his mind but to win. The batter was out before the ball left the pitcher's hand. As he was throwing that last pitch, I felt as if someone had lit a fire under me. I asked myself, "What is there in my life that I would like to give my all for? What do I want to put my energy into, with all my heart? How do I want to win?"

All I could think of was living for God; walking in dignity and mastery; forgiving at every opportunity; and letting each moment of my life radiate joy. If my presence on the planet could bring greater love into the world, there is nothing more I could ever want.

### Stand True To Yourself

You, too, have a purpose. There is something that you believe in, a vision that stimulates you, a function that makes your heart content as you fill it. The form of your ministry does not matter as much as your energy, investment, focus, and commitment to your goal. You are sure to achieve the goal that your heart truly values.

We are spiritual beings. The important element of our life is the spirit in which we do what we do. Our acts are valuable not because of the way they appear, but for the depth of spirit that we bring to what we create. We are here to develop our song until it truly says what we want the world to hear; to establish our relationships in a way that brings peace and healing to everyone involved. We find fulfillment only when we stand and live for what we truly believe.

*Major League.* We are all born to play in the majors. A lot of us have been bouncing around the minors for a long time, considering ourselves second-rate players, letting our God-endowed skills go undeveloped because we believed that we just didn't have what it takes. But like that season's Indians, you don't know that you have what it takes until you take what you have and use it.

Because we are major leaguers, it doesn't behoove us to play in the minors any longer. We are major league lovers, major league thinkers, children of a major league God who thrills to see us win at the sport of being who we really are. Yes, we've made lots of errors. But so what?

In the spiritual game you don't get to walk off the field until you've won the pennant. The season goes on until you've mastered the sport.

In the God League the goal is endless love. It's about being bigger than we thought we were, and forgiving what we thought we couldn't. It's about seeing the best in ourselves and everyone we meet. It's about wholeheartedly delivering that magnificent vision to a world in sore need of greater faith. If we wait for someone else to do it for us, it might not happen. But if we step out in faith, courage, and commitment, it will. There is no other choice but to win, and no other league to play in but the majors.

# Section Five

# *Living the Vision*

# REAL
# VISION

*I thought it ironic that it would be a blind man who would be my teacher of vision. I realized that it is possible to have one's eyes open and yet walk in darkness, and to have one's eyes closed and see all the universe.*

Joybubbles is a very unusual guy. He operates the "Zzzzerific Fun Line" in Minneapolis, a telephone service through which many people call to chat, joke, and listen to his stories and songs. He chose that name for his service because he wanted to be the last listing in the Minneapolis phone book. (He read in the Bible, "He who is last shall later be first.")

Known to some of his friends simply as Joe, this man has an amazing sense of seeing the goodness in life. This is especially poignant because, physically speaking, Joe is blind. If there is anyone who ever lived to prove that true seeing does not come through the physical eyes, it is Joe.

To me, Joe is a teacher of the power of innocence. Although he is about 40 years of age—physically speaking—Joybubbles has chosen to live in the playfulness of a five-year-old.

One day while at a retreat I was walking to the cafeteria for lunch, discussing metaphysical matters with some friends. My attention was distracted by a large being with a red t-shirt lying under a tree. It was Joybubbles. He had decided that the lecture schedule was a little too much for a five-year-old, and that he needed to be in the healing power of nature. There he lay with his stuffed doll, "Mr. Squish," on his tummy, and his head propped up against the roots of a great tree. At Joe's fingertips was a cassette player for the blind, with a chorus of sweet voices singing to him "I love you" in a symphony of gentle intonations. Joe was engaged in the art of giving himself love—a gift that many of us who are often distracted by the sights of the outer world do not allow ourselves to enjoy.

I decided that Joe's method of coming to God playfully was more real in that moment than my theological debate or my need for lunch. Here was real spiritual food, and I was not about to miss the feast! I laid down on the ground next to Joe and put my head on his shoulder. I found it soft and welcoming. True to his custom, Joybubbles instantly made up a silly song about the moment. I laughed. I saw that in his innocent playfulness, Joe had escaped the nets of the mind that have so often bound me. Joe turned the tape over, and together we heard a half-hour of outrageous laughter. I remembered a quote from Master Hilarion, who noted that "the halls of heaven ring with the laughter of the saints."

The last night of the retreat, I participated in a healing service. As I stood in the row of healers, I was delighted to see Joe in the line of participants on their way to sit in the empty chairs in front of us. There they would receive prayer and the laying on of hands. "Psst!" I called to him. "Joybubbles—sit here!" I tried to disguise my voice so he would not know it was me.

Joe, true to the surrender of a child, happily complied. He sat in the chair in front of me and I placed my hands on his shoulders. I took a few breaths and began to tune in to Spirit, inviting God's healing essence to flow through me. But my meditation was interrupted by some words that Joe was speaking. Wondering if he was talking to me, I lowered my head and put my ear next to his mouth.

"Thank you, wonderful, wonderful God, for all my blessings," I heard him say. "I must be the most fortunate person in the entire world. Oh, my precious God—you have given me gift after gift, and I feel so much joy welling up within me that I can't possibly contain it all. Thank you, God, for all of your rich, rich blessings."

I felt stunned. Joe was not talking to me; I don't even think he knew I was his prayer partner. Joe was talking to God, and he was gushing forth appreciation from the deepest well of his heart. He was not asking God for anything, and he was not saying affirmations in an effort to convince himself that they were true. Joe was already in a state of appreciative ecstasy, the natural result of loving with a childlike heart.

The purity and innocence of Joe's exclamations cut like a knife through the walls I had built around me. His words touched my soul directly. It was almost too much for me to handle. A spring of tears welled up inside me and poured down my cheeks.

With my head against Joe's cheek, together we wept and prayed. If there was ever a moment that God was present between two brothers, that was it. Although I was in the healer's position, I was being healed. Here was a man who perhaps had never seen a sunset, the morning dew, or the stars in the nighttime sky. Perhaps he had never seen anything at all with his physical eyes. Yet his enthusiasm and sense of the preciousness of his life was far greater than that of many of us who take physical beauty for granted.

I thought of the things that I complain about, and they all seemed so petty, so trivial. In that moment I realized that happiness is a choice.

Joybubbles has clearly chosen to be happy; he does not let the outer world dictate his aliveness. He sees no outer world. But he does see a lot. His vision is quite clear. He sees God. Late that night, as I packed my bags to leave the conference, I thought it ironic that it would be a blind man who would be my teacher of vision. I thought of the verse in the song, "Amazing Grace," which extols, "I once was blind, but now I see." I realized that it is possible to have one's eyes open and yet walk in darkness, and to have one's eyes closed and see all the universe.

# THE GARDEN

*You cannot see God and forget about it.*
*You cannot feel perfection and then*
*take refuge in half-hearted living.*
*When you have made the choice to see*
*and be only love, you are committed to*
*going all the way home.*

Whon I was in the fifth grade I read in my social studies book that the Garden of Eden was in a place called Mesopotamia, a "fertile crescent" which spawned human life. Here, another book said, Adam and Eve lived, played, brought us the original fruitarian diet, kicked the designer fig-leaf market off to a flying start, and eventually learned to feel guilty for it all. Scientists, the teacher said, were still researching to pinpoint the exact location of the garden.

I heard nothing more about the Garden of Eden for the next few decades. I assumed that the scientists had either not found it and were too embarrassed to admit it, or they *had* found it and never returned to tell about it. But no matter what had happened to them, something inside me advised me not to sit around and wait for the explorers' findings. Instead, that inner voice counseled, I needed to *become* the explorer. Peace, I began to see, could not be found for me by someone else. The only way I would be able to enter the Garden of Eden would be to find it myself.

Last year I discovered it. Not in Mesopotamia, but within my own heart. For years I had been hearing my spiritual guide, Hilda, explain to our class, "The Garden of Eden is not a place—it is a *consciousness*. Adam and Eve are not just historical figures. They are you and me."

A bell rang within me. I felt the kind of resonance I experience when something I need to know has just been said. A wave of excitement rippled up my spine. My soul thrilled to the possibilities!

Then Hilda led us into a deep meditation. "Look within yourself," she guided. "Inside you is all the good, peace, and plenty you have sought in the outer world. Dive deep into your heart. There you will find the Garden of God."

She gave this instruction with such conviction and knowingness that I knew she was speaking from her own experience. If there was such a place, I wanted to see it and walk in it. This was the adventure I had been seeking all my life!

I decided to take the leap. To find the inner paradise I needed to leave behind everything in the outer world. I put aside my body, the calls of my senses, and the burning urges of physical existence. I dove within, eager to set out on the odyssey of the heart. I was ready to learn the truth about what lies within me.

When I looked within myself, I found something more beautiful than anything my eyes had ever beheld. Paradise was rich and green, sparkling with a song of melodies spun of a loveliness my ears had heard only in ancient dreams. Sunlight poured over waterfalls flowing into shimmering brooks. Fragrant wildflowers colored the landscape. I beheld a world that brought me refreshment and renewal.

I felt a sense of welcome and homecoming. Good was apparent everywhere, and limitation nowhere. Here was a land of perfect peace, untainted by mortal thought. Here was a fountain of endless blessings.

I entered the inner garden where the first Child of God was born. Here was the breath of life itself, the heaven that kissed the earth into the first morning. It was the reason for every act of giving, the source of light in a child's eyes, and the promise of forgiveness that no dark dream can destroy. It was the pure joy of God in a world the soul's senses could touch and feel.

An inner voice spoke: *"This is the garden of healing. It is an oasis in your consciousness, a realm within the mansion of your soul. This garden is a very real place, indestructible by the illusions of appearances. You can come here and renew yourself whenever you need and choose. It is a gift from God to you; more truly, it is God in a form that your divine senses can know and find peace in. Eternal love is in you, and you have found it."*

I remained in the garden for what seemed to be a long, long time. By the clocks of earth it was perhaps just a few moments. By the measure of heaven it was eternity. The moment came for me to return. I opened my eyes, and saw the room where I had begun my sacred journey. Physically it was the same place, but it did not look the same to me. The room was permeated with gentleness and a sense of blessing. It was different because I was different. The world had become new because I saw it through the eyes of innocence.

The meditation was over, but the journey had just begun. My glimpse of heaven has remained with me wherever I go. You cannot see God and forget about it. You cannot feel perfection and then take refuge in half-hearted living. You can deny the garden and cover it over, but eventually the grass will push its way through the concrete and remind you that nature is more powerful than manipulation. You may retreat into the cave of fear, but you cannot convince yourself that you do not know what you know. When you have made the choice to see and be only love, a divine door closes behind you, and you are committed to going all the way home.

Now when I see the earth coming green in the springtime, the season calls to me as a reminder of the garden I saw. Each seed I plant in the ground is a symbol of the seeds I sow in my heart. The seeds we sow are fed by the thoughts we think, protected by the words we offer one another, and watered by the gentleness with which honor our innocence. We *are* Adam and Eve. The garden grows within. There is nowhere to go but home.

# THE HEAVEN GAME

*Heaven begins within our thoughts, and
finds its way to expression in our life.
Why would I need to close my eyes to
find heaven, if I were seeing it all around me?*

The airplane touched down to the Newark runway at 9 o'clock on Sunday night. I was sure glad to be home. It had been a long weekend of traveling and workshops, and I looked forward to stretching out and catching up on listening to my favorite music. My friend Anne would be waiting for me at the gate, and it would be good to see her.

When I reached the lobby, Anne was not there. I waited five, ten, fifteen minutes. Still no sign. Where was she?

I phoned her house and, to my surprise, Anne answered. "Where are you?" I asked. (Actually, it was a rhetorical question. I already knew the answer, but it was not the one I wanted to hear.)

"I'm home," she replied brightly. "Where are you?"

"I'm at Newark Airport."

"Nooooo!"

"That's what this sign here says."

"But you're not coming in until tomorrow night."

I looked at my ticket. "The ticket says I'm here tonight."

"The message from your office said Monday night."

"I don't think the pilot got the same message."

"OK—Hang in there...I'll be right there."

Right there meant at least 45 minutes. I felt annoyed. It was hot and smoggy, and there were great masses of humanity moving all about. This was definitely not my idea of a happy homecoming. "Why is this happening, God?" I questioned. "What am I going to do in Newark Airport for almost an hour?"

The Voice came loud and clear: *"Why not practice being happy?"*

"Yeah, that's easy for You to say," I retorted. "You get to hang out on some celestial cloud, listening to Andreas Vollenwieder music and watching Charlton Heston movies—You don't have to sit in Newark airport on a Sunday night."

*"What makes you think that's not heaven?"*

"Now, really, God, you're stretching it on that one."

*"Am I?"*

"Of course You are. If You're so great, why didn't You have Anne here on time?"

"Listen, son," the Big Air Traffic Controller went on. (It reminded me of one of those talks Ward Cleaver would have with Beaver.)

*"Remember the Course in Miracles lesson, 'I could see peace instead of this'?"*

(Why is it that God always has to hit you with the truth when you least want to hear it?)

"Sure, I remember."

*"Well, here's your chance to practice. Imagine that you are in heaven now."*

"You sure do have a great imagination."

*"I know—That's how I created the entire universe. Not a bad production, wouldn't you agree?"*

I had to agree. I had my assignment.

So I decided to play a little game while I waited. I decided to imagine that I was in heaven, and everything I saw happening before me was actually happening in heaven.

I saw families greeting their children at the gate. What a wonderful scene—families reuniting in heaven! (So those 1940's films were right!) My heart felt warm.

I watched the porters picking up baggage off the carousel and delivering it to waiting cars and limousines. I noticed they were smiling. "Wow," I exclaimed to myself, "...they are assisting people with their arrival into heaven—what a great job!"

Then I noticed several people standing at the rent-a-car desks, making arrangements to pick up transportation. "How exciting!" I remarked. "These folks have arrived in heaven and they're about to take a tour and then find their homes of eternal peace!"

Before long I was in a state of deep tranquility. The flight attendant had announced, "Welcome to New Jersey," but I was beginning to see that was but a part of the whole picture.

Sitting there, in what seemed to be Newark Airport, I felt lifted into an exquisitely tranquil meditation—with my eyes open. Why would I need to close my eyes to find heaven, if I were seeing it all around me?

My reveries were interrupted by the sensation of a hand on my shoulder. In blissful slow motion, I looked up to see Anne standing there. "Hi!" she smiled.

Could it have been 45 minutes?

"Ready to go?" she asked, car keys jingling in her hand.

"Sit down," I invited her. "This is a fabulous place!"

I have said many things that surprised Anne, but this one really startled her. Amazed, she sat down.

I took her hand and explained the heaven game to her. At first she looked at me incredulously, but soon she began to enjoy the idea. Of course, she was happy to play. There we sat, unreasonably peaceful in a place where God is not usually remembered.

Then came the icing on the cake. A rather harried fellow approached us and asked if we wouldn't mind watching his bags for a few minutes while he made a phone call. Already in heaven, we had no place to go, so we were happy to tell him, "Sure." A short while later he returned and thanked us profusely for our help.

Then it occurred to me that we had just brought heaven to earth. Because we were in a heavenly state of consciousness, we served a brother and made his life easier. If we were in a state of fear or impatience, we might have said no or acquiesced begrudgingly. But we were at peace, and in that consciousness it was our joy to help him.

I saw that we had actually *created* heaven in Newark airport. And we saw it manifest in a very practical way. Heaven begins within our thoughts, and finds its way to expression in our life. In Newark Airport, as it is in heaven.

# DESOLATION TO DEVELOPMENT

*Find your Source, live from it, keep your
heart open, and laugh generously. These
are the maxims of the peaceful teacher,
the tools of a gentle healer. Think with God,
and you will make the desert bloom.*

Recently I visited the Hyatt Regency Waikoloa, the fantastic luxury hotel on the western shore of the Big Island of Hawaii. The hotel is billed as the most fabulous resort on earth. I believe it may be so.

Built at a cost of $365 million and sprawling over 62 acres, this playground retreat is a Disneyland for adults. Three elegant towers containing 1,250 rooms afford views of the Hawaiian sunset over the ocean on one side, and awe-inspiring volcanic mountains on the other.

Upon our arrival, we had a choice of being taken to our room via boat or monorail. We chose the boat, and we were delighted to find the intricate system of waterways blessed by stately Buddhas meditating along the route. When we arrived at our room we stepped out onto the balcony and discovered we were directly overlooking the dolphin lagoon. What a treat to awaken in the middle of the night and hear the dolphins talking and playing!

What inspired me most about the Hyatt Regency Waikoloa is its location. The resort is built in the middle of a lava wilderness. The Waikoloa region of the Big Island is a mass of brittle black volcanic rock in shapes and forms that are almost impossible to walk on. Much of the area is as stark as the dark side of the moon.

The Hyatt visionaries did not allow geography to stand between them and their dream. When the hotel chain's expansion committee saw the site, they saw not desolation, but development. That fabulous resort began with one free-thinking person who had a grand idea. And because ideas are more powerful than matter (if you don't mind, it doesn't matter), the earth gave way to heaven. I remember one sage's lesson that a person with spiritual vision "sees a sermon in a stone."

The Hyatt developers brought in *everything* to make the resort the wonder that it is: the soil, a thousand full-grown palm trees, hundreds of exotic birds, the dolphins, and the Buddhas. The many waterfalls on the property, the canals, and the dolphin lagoon were all designed and manufactured by people. Someone with a big idea invited thousands of co-workers to play with him, and together they literally made a desert bloom.

What an example of the power of creative vision! To me, creativity is the reflection of God's presence in the world. There are two mighty gifts that demonstrate that a human being is thinking with God. One is *vision*—the ability to see good, beauty, and healing where they seem to be absent; the other is *creativity*—the opening to allow the vision to come to life through action.

I am inspired to take areas of my life that seem to be desolate, and make them bloom. I am becoming more sensitive to thoughts that there is a lack in my life—time, money, or love, for example. My challenge is to take such areas of arid thinking and develop them with consciousness to create gardens where there once seemed to be only wasteland.

## Mastery through Creativity

Everything comes from God, and everything is for healing. Consider desolate times, for example. As I look back over my life, I consider the times when I seemed to be wandering in the desert, parched of spirit and painfully separated from God. I recognize that I have become much stronger as a result of the spiritual muscle I developed through such trying times. I see that these difficult periods were always followed by awakening, spurts of accelerated growth, and important changes for the better. Don't fight hard times—just keep blessing them! When you realize that they *are* a blessing, you will wonder how you ever lived with the unconsciousness that created your difficulties. Problems are not punishments; they are gifts. Dilemmas are God's way of getting us out of the mire and onto solid ground. Every minus is simply half of a plus that is waiting for a stroke of vertical awareness.

Desolation forces us to be creative. I am happiest when I am creating. There is something about giving birth to new ideas that is enlivening for me. When I am creating, I feel I am fulfilling God's purpose for me on earth. When I am not creating, I wonder what I am doing here. The creative urge moves me to want to get up in the morning, to travel, to meet people, to take risks, to leap into the unknown. Real creativity never feels like a dangerous risk. The same God who gives us a good idea will see it, and us, through. Problems are a call not for complaints, but for creativity. Where there is creativity, God is very present. Truly creative people are the masters of the circumstances in their life. No one can be in the creative process and be a victim of circumstances. Creative people make circumstances; circumstances don't make them.

## How to Make a Desert Bloom

I was delighted by the character in the movie, *Tucker—The Man and*

*His Dream.* The film is a true story of Preston Tucker who, in the 1940's, invented an automobile with many features that have become standard equipment on the cars of the 80's and 90's. His "car of the future" embodied many advanced designs such as seatbelts, a pop-out windshield, front disc brakes, and fuel injection, to name a few. Preston Tucker was far ahead of his time.

Although he was just one man with a "wild" scheme, Preston succeeded in obtaining money, facilities, and labor to produce 150 prototype automobiles. Soon the prevailing powers in the automotive industry were threatened by Tucker's inventions, and they did everything possible to squelch his efforts. Ultimately he was brought to trial on trumped-up charges.

As he sat in the courtroom, facing accusations that could have put him in jail for many years, Tucker was doodling. At first I couldn't figure out what he was drawing, but the final scene of the movie revealed the answer. After he was found not guilty, Tucker set out on his next invention: a new kind of refrigerator, one which would revolutionize the industry.

Just think of it: Here was a man facing serious punishment, being crucified by people who felt threatened by his innovations, seeing his work shot to pieces before his eyes—and he was creating! What a fantastic model of the nature and power of the creative mind! He did not waste a moment in fear or resistance. All of Tucker's energies were flowing toward more, bigger, better, and greater.

Why? Because he had to create. Because he saw something more than others saw. Because he wanted to improve the world in the way that he was personally inspired to do. Because nothing gave him greater joy than to make the unseen seen. Because only those who see the invisible can do the impossible.

It was the same vision, imaginative power, and persistence that made the Hyatt Waikoloa rise from the most literal of ashes. That selfsame spirit that has the power to make an noble edifice rise from the ashes of our lives.

It does not matter what has been or what you have done. What you think you have done is only your concept, not God's vision of who you are and what you can do. Like the Hyatt developers and Preston Tucker, you have the vision and the power to bring wondrous gifts to the earth. They may not be resorts or automobiles, but they will be real and personally meaningful for you. That is all that God asks of you—to do what you believe in and walk your path with dignity and integrity. That is how the world will change. The world will become new because you have become new. Find your Source, live from it, keep your heart open, and laugh generously. These are the maxims of the peaceful teacher, the tools of a gentle healer. Think with God, and you will make the desert bloom.

# IGOR'S CHOICE

*I see how joyful this man is, how much
good he has found in his world.
In the midst of a grey, concrete Moscow,
Igor has found a reason to celebrate
his life. Then it dawns on me.
Igor has chosen to be happy.*

Just having returned from my third visit to the Soviet Union, I am excited to report that amazing changes are taking place there. The country is donning a new face. We are witnessing the miracle that many of us have been praying for.

A stirring moment came for me one evening when we turned on the television to watch a news program. There we saw Premier Gorbachov meeting in his office with 15 American teachers of Russian language. The tone of the gathering was light and friendly, very family-like. Mr. Gorbachov was genuinely interested in getting to know these people. He asked who the youngest person in the group was. A woman sheepishly rose, and the premier comforted her with a gentle joke and invited her to ask whatever she liked.

Our Soviet friend Elena, who was watching the program with us, translated one of his statements: "I refuse to agree with anyone who says that America is an aggressive nation." Later I was told that Mr. Gorbachov has announced that his personal objective is the removal of all nuclear weapons from the planet by the year 2000. Clearly this leader is a man of peace, and he needs and deserves our prayers and support.

Sweeping transformations are occurring in our sister country. For the first time in Soviet history, democratic elections are being held, and there are more candidates than posts to be filled. The policy of *glasnost* (openness) is moving so rapidly that many of the old rules are swirling about like brittle leaves in a gusty wind; no one knows exactly where they will land.

My friend Bob, an American living in Moscow, works as a translator for the *Moscow News*. During my visit Bob took out the current week's copy of that newspaper and pointed: "Here, look at the letters to the editor on page two." We found a letter from a Russian man questioning why it is so difficult for Soviet citizens to obtain visas to visit other countries. "Even just a few months ago you would not have seen an article like this," Bob explained. "And next week there will be an astounding article on corruption in the police department."

The desire and need for personal expression, like the grass of freedom that has been tarred over by political repression, is growing through the cracks and making way for new life. Russian women are dressing more gaily; whereas just a few years ago most clothing was grey and drab, Soviet women are now sporting colorful prints and even bold pinks and yellows. A Soviet friend told us that until this year a central committee determined what fashions (which we in the west would not consider very fashionable at all) were to be manufactured for the country. Now stores may order styles and patterns based upon customer request.

The stirrings of free enterprise in Russia are being felt: Some of our tour group made an expedition to Moscow's first pizza parlor; Russian citizens are now able to obtain mortgages; and last year the first Soviet MasterCard was issued. (Perhaps the cold war will end not through arms or negotiations, but through plastic!)

Soviet people of spiritual orientation are feeling the first rays of the sunlight of artistic freedom. My friend Slava is a young mystical artist, passionate with enthusiasm for his art. When I met Slava in his Leningrad apartment last October, I was deeply inspired by the depth and richness of his paintings. He told me sadly that there was no way for him to show his work in public. "The committee does not give permission to display art like mine," Slava explained.

When I saw him this August, Slava smiled and took me to a gallery in the central park of Leningrad. There his art was being shown along with that of several other spiritual artists. Something very good and Godly is happening in Russia.

## The Gift of Blessing

On the last night of our visit to Moscow, a small group from our tour took a cab to meet Igor Mikhailusenko, a poet. We arrived at his flat on the sixth floor of an apartment house over a *beriozka*, a small state-operated gift store near the heart of Moscow. Igor's apartment is small, but very homey. He has been there for 12 years. As Igor greeted us at the door, I was instantly touched by his warmth. He was bubbling with delight in having us as his guests.

Igor lost his parents and both of his legs at the age of 10, when a Nazi bomb fell on his home. He has since learned to maneuver with artificial limbs extremely well, to the point of being quite agile. I was amazed to watch him scurry about his flat in his zeal to entertain us properly. Igor disappeared into the kitchen, still talking, and emerged with a bottle of Pepsi, four glasses, and a tray of hard candy—his red-carpet welcome for important guests! We were honored. We found the treats to be a splendid feast, largely because of the love and sense of caring with which they were offered.

We spent the entire evening looking through a scrapbook of Igor's poetry and photographs. He writes about joy and celebrates the goodness of life. Some of his poetry has been published in various Russian and international poetic magazines. We were touched to the point of tears.

For many years Igor has been trying to obtain permission to visit the United States and other countries. Repeatedly he has made application, to no avail. He does not want to defect—his dream is to learn more about the world, himself, and life, and then come home and share what he has learned with his fellow citizens. "I trust that somehow the doors will be opened!" Igor gleefully states. I am amazed at how happy this man is.

I look at Igor's living room walls. Physically, he has practically nothing. One of his treasures is the jacket of a 1950's 45 rpm record of *Boney Maroney*, artfully displayed near the center of his living room wall. To Igor it is a prize.

I see how joyful this man is, how much good he has found in his world. In the midst of a grey, concrete Moscow, Igor has found a reason to celebrate his life. Then it dawns on me. Igor has *chosen* to be happy. He has made an inner decision to enjoy every moment. He does not allow outer circumstances to bring him down—he has chosen to bring outer circumstances up. I remember the *Course in Miracles* lessons that I am affected only by my thoughts, and I can choose to see differently. To me, Igor is a glorious model of a human being who has chosen to see beauty everywhere.

Igor takes out one more poem and asks if we would like to hear it before we leave. Of course we would. We listen and we learn. I see. Here, in Russia, I learn how a man can find paradise within himself.

## DECLARATION OF LOVE

### by Igor Mikhailusenko

*I am a Man. In love! In love!*
*The planet's bells ring out above!*
*The bells of Spring, they ring and ring!*
*On Earth nought harmful can evil bring!*

*In love with all the heavenly height,*
*In love with dreams in winging flight,*
*In love with all the blooming flowers,*
*Where you go wandering hours and hours!*

*In love with the water's expanse of blue,*
*Where steamers white go streaming through,*
*In love with forests robed in green,*
*Where birds are heard and gladly seen.*

*In love with earthly people so,*
*With flocks of swans, as white as snow,*
*In love with ancient mountain peaks*
*Where Eternity still spaces seeks!*

*In love with all which round me lies,*
*And with the dear, so-near-me skies.*
*In love with the gleam of a distant star*
*To which the road is hard and far...*

*And therefore I must simply say,*
*"I'm burning with new love today!"*

A note to readers:

A few months after writing this account, I received a telephone call from Igor. He was in Philadelphia, en route to visit a spiritual commune in New Mexico. When Igor said, "I am sure the doors will open!" he wasn't kidding!

# TRIBUTE TO A GREAT SOUL

*She saw something greater in me than
I saw in myself. In many ways I didn't
think I was any good as a person.
But she knew better, and she never once
agreed with my doubts. All she
agreed with was my divinity.*

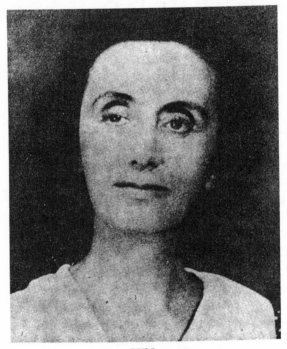

*Hilda*

S he was consistently loving, dynamically powerful, and utterly unpredictable. She was obligated to no one except God, and she served everyone as God. She taught, counseled, and healed thousands, available for lengths of time and depths of intensity beyond what seemed humanly possible, and she accepted no money or fame for all that she gave.

Recently Hilda Charlton, my beloved spiritual teacher, left the physical life to enter the world of higher light. As my way of paying tribute to Hilda's presence in my life, I am moved to share some of the images and feelings that call to me in reflection of the many gifts I received from this angel of friendship and guidance.

It was just before New Year's when some friends invited me to Hilda's class in a small gymnasium on the grounds of St. Luke's Church in Greenwich Village. The room was filled wall to wall with spiritual seekers. They were sitting on the floor, in chairs, on the stage, on the tops of cabinets, and in places where I would never have believed a person could sit for hours. (Perhaps that was the first miracle.) Some had little photographs of their guru and were burning incense before them. On the large altar in front of the room were huge pictures of Sai Baba, Jesus, and other beloved gurus. It was an unusual, vibrant scene. I was enticed.

Sitting next to Hilda was a beautiful young singer named Mirabai. As Hilda led us into meditation, Mirabai's voice wafted in and out of Hilda's words. The tones were so etheric that they seemed to call golden angels into the room—a perfect complement to Hilda's poetry. Later Mirabai gathered steam and belted a soulful song of joy: *"O, mama, what you've done to me! Turned your sheepish little daughter into the Rock of Gibraltar—O, mama, what you've done to me!"*

I had no idea that this would be the song of my transformation, as well. I wouldn't have guessed that Hilda would become my personal teacher and spiritual guide for the next 14 years. Over those years Hilda became precious to me in a way unlike anyone I had ever known.

Her history was certainly quite different than mine, yet there was something curiously attractive about this unusual woman. She wore an Indian sari in New York movie theatres, quoted the *National Enquirer*, and enjoyed Bette Midler concerts. She offered a compassionate shoulder to prostitutes and drug addicts, and dined with diplomats and celebrities.

179

One night I saw her wiping down the counter of a pizza parlor on the outskirts of Harlem, a business she and her students managed in order to sponsor orphans in South America. The next day she was healing one of the stars of *Saturday Night Live* over the telephone. She was unlike anyone, and like everyone. She was Hilda.

That first meeting was a sweet mystery for me. I couldn't quite decide if it was a class, a lecture, a church service, or a comedy routine. Whatever it was, it was light, joyful, powerful, and from the heart. Whatever it was, I wanted more. I came back the next week, and again I was touched. The weeks turned into months, the months into years, and the years into a new life.

A few months after I met Hilda, I was at a screening of *Sunseed*, a pioneering new age motion picture in which Hilda and a number of other popular spiritual teachers were featured. The movie ended, the lights came on, and there sitting across from me in the theatre was Hilda. (It seemed as if I would always run into her either when I least expected to see her or when I most needed to be with her.) Sheepishly I said "hello," wondering if I was being presumptuous to approach her. To my happy surprise, Hilda lit up to see me. She greeted me with a huge "Hello, darling!" I could hardly believe the love that she was giving me—I didn't even think she knew me, and she acknowledged me as if she were looking into the face of the Christ. Perhaps she was.

That was to become Hilda's great gift to me over the next two decades—it seemed that she always saw more in me than I saw in myself. Constantly, sometimes relentlessly, with uncompromising purpose, Hilda acknowledged only the greatness in me and all of her students.

One evening after class I walked up to Hilda and asked her a question about the lesson. She put the question aside and quickly went to what she had to tell me.

"How long have you been with me, kid?" (She called everyone "kid." People 70, 80, and 90 years old were her kids as well.)

"About three years."

"Well, I think you have been receiving long enough—It's time you started giving out. Why don't you start a little meditation group at your house? It doesn't have to be fancy; you can just put a little ad in the local paper saying, '*People desiring spiritual support and uplifting group meditation are welcome,'* or something like that. Do you know anyone who plays the guitar?"

"It's funny you should ask that—I play the guitar."

"Well, then, it's time for you to get started—you'll do fine!" Then she turned to the next person in line. She had an amazing way of saying just what she needed to say—no more, no less.

Years passed. The meditation group grew from a seed to a flower to a mighty tree. Day by day, moment by moment, Hilda crept into my heart, becoming to me a teacher and a friend unlike any I had ever known or expected.

No one knew her age or her birthday. (I didn't really want to know, either.) She was timelessly youthful and ever-present. I don't know if *she* knew her age or birthday. She was always *now*. Once, while telling a story about her early days, Hilda started to say, "That was in my time..." Then she stopped in mid-sentence and corrected herself: "But I can't really say that was my time, kids—my time is *now!*"

Hilda used everything that happened to her as a doorway to come closer to God. Then she used the strength she had gained from her experience, and offered healing to those who were struggling with the fears that she had overcome.

As a young girl, Hilda received visions and visitations from Jesus, angels, and spiritual masters. One day while she was meditating in her room, a yogi in a loincloth appeared to her. This holy man was sitting under a palm tree and making various hand motions; he spoke only in a kind of a grunt. Hilda knew not who this was, but she did know that they had an important destiny together.

Hilda became a classical dancer of remarkable grace, creating dances which brought a vibration of tremendous spiritual power to those who observed and felt them. "The Dance of Life" and "The Dance of St. Francis" became vehicles through which she offered blessing. For "The Dance of the Far Eastern Masters," Hilda found a large metal funnel and fashioned it into an elegant Siamese crown. That was the way she did things—simply, cleverly, in her own way.

One evening Hilda came to class glowing. "Kids, I had the greatest miracle today!" she announced. "I was looking for living room curtains for a long time, and they were all so expensive; none of them really suited me. So I just let go and decided to trust God. Then, today I was in Lambston's, and there I found them—in the form of shower curtains! And at half the price! I took them home and put them up, and you know what? They're perfect! This afternoon God confirmed that He wanted them there. A guest complimented me on my beautiful living room curtains! I tell you, God always works!" The lesson that night was called, "Take what'cha got and make what'cha want."

*Hilda performing the
Dance of the Mayan Priestess*

Hilda joined a dance troupe and set off to India for a six-month tour. The six months turned into eighteen years. During that time she became a yogi, a renunciate, a disciple of God. She threw herself totally on the mercy of the Holy Spirit. Sometimes she had no food and sometimes she walked with holes in her shoes. Hilda trekked to the top of the Himalayas and there found a yogi in a cave. He took out some parchments made of tea leaves, on which her horoscope was written. The yogi described her life to her, and told her much that was to come. The parchment, he explained, had been inscribed thousands of years earlier. Perhaps my destiny with her was written into the stars in the same way.

While in southern India Hilda made a pilgrimage to see the great Swami Nityananda, the guru of the well-known Swami Muktananda. As she approached the temple, all Hilda could think and feel was, "My beloved, my beloved... I'm going to see my beloved!" Though she had never seen him, she knew that something mighty was about to happen.

Hilda entered the sanctuary and there, to her amazement, sat the same yogi who had appeared to her in her room years earlier. He motioned to her with the same hand gestures and communicated with the same sounds he used in her Oakland apartment many years before, half a world away. "I knew I was home," Hilda told us with the softest heart I can imagine.

Hilda became a devoted student of Nityananda. She would stand in line for hours to walk past him and be in his physical presence for a brief moment, during which he never spoke except in gestures and his guttural sounds. "And in that one moment," Hilda shared, "the whole universe was given unto me." It was that universe that she passed on to the rest of us.

Hilda spent many years in India, hiking, fasting, praying, renouncing physical comforts, and studying closely with the great gurus such as Yogananda and Sai Baba. Then one day she was sitting on the banks of the sacred Ganges, with her feet dangling in the water. Before her, in her mind's eye, came the faces of many young people calling to her. She did not understand the vision, but she knew she had to return to America. She decided to come back for a few months.

When she returned to New York, Hilda found a different world. It was the late 60's and she discovered that there had been a major shift in consciousness. As a young spiritual seeker Hilda had been teased and ridiculed for her "way-out" beliefs—such as yoga, spiritual healing, and the reality of worlds beyond this one. Now millions of people were studying yoga, seeking meditation instruction, and opening their minds and hearts to a higher life.

Hilda told us about the moment she realized there had been a great change: "One afternoon I looked out my living room window and there, down in the street, I saw hundreds of young people with long hair, marching and chanting, *'Dump the Hump!...Dump the Hump!'* 'What could possibly be happening?' I wondered. Later I found out that they were campaigning against Hubert Humphrey in that election. The politics were not so important to me, but one thing I knew—It was not the same world I had left two decades earlier."

Casually, informally, naturally, a few people began to discover the love and power that Hilda emanated. A handful of seekers sat and chatted with her in her living room for a few hours, and when they arrived home they discovered they were healed. They came back with a few friends, and those friends brought their friends. The small group grew into a class, and so it all began in a living room on West End Avenue in upper Manhattan. When the living room became too crowded, a larger meeting place was found, and that gave way to the gym at St. Luke's where I first met her. Later we moved to the Cathedral of St. John the Divine, where hundreds of people came each week to be touched and receive the kind of love that they were not finding in their daily lives. Some came nearly every week for many years, as I did, and some came only once. Yet each one received what he or she needed, each one saw greater possibilities for their life, and each one was changed.

One evening a group of us were at a party with Hilda, and I played a song on the guitar. "That was wonderful, darling!" Hilda exclaimed. "Why don't you bring your guitar to class next week and play for the group?"

I gulped. "The group" meant three or four hundred people. "Why, sure, Hilda—I'd be happy to," I answered, attempting to sound confident, but feeling nervous. She smiled. She knew I was scared. She also knew I could do it. She always knew what I could do, especially when I didn't.

Before long I was playing the guitar and singing at all of Hilda's classes and informal gatherings. One evening at our farm in upstate New York, Hilda asked me to sit next to her chair and just sing and play for her all evening. She asked as if it was a gift to her, and it was really a gift to me. You see, I never really thought I was any good as a singer or guitarist. But she saw something greater in me than I saw in myself. In many ways I didn't think I was any good as a person. But she knew better, and she never once agreed with my doubts. All she agreed with was my divinity.

There were many more moments such as that one, many times Hilda somehow got my soul to stretch, to become bigger, to become more of who I now know myself to be. Sometimes she was sharp and confrontive, but most of the time she was very gentle with me. Hilda once said that every person has strayed from God in one of two directions: arrogance or unworthiness. The arrogant people she would cut to shreds in a moment, and the unworthy ones she would cuddle and nurture and support. She gave each one what they needed, and that is why lives changed in her presence. We learned from her words and her example. Her life was her message. She was to each of us what we needed her to be.

One winter I was facing the most painful time in my life. My mother had just been diagnosed with terminal cancer, my girlfriend and I were breaking up, I had contracted a staph infection, it was the dead of winter, and I was alone. I went to the doctor for some surgery which turned out to be extremely painful, and on the drive to the pharmacy for some antibiotics and pain-killers, I hit a snowstorm. The world around me was blanketed with pure white, but inside I was feeling dark and bleak.

I reached the drug store and pushed myself toward the prescription counter. Everyone in line took one look at me and stepped aside. Being so distraught, I had brought no money with me. The pharmacist surveyed my condition and let me take the drugs on a promise. I drove home in the snow, feeling despair and discouragement.

I stopped at the entrance of my driveway to check the mail. When I opened the mailbox door, there was a letter from Hilda. It was addressed to *"Alan-ji Cohen."* The suffix *"ji"* is an Indian term of endearment and respect commonly used when addressing masters and honored persons. I could hardly believe my eyes. I opened the letter and read,

*Dearest Alan,*
*I am so proud of you and what you are doing for God. It is wonderful...Remain humble through all activities and know deep within that you do nothing and He does all. That is the secret of life...God is all...I love you Alan for your sweetness and humbleness and for all you are doing...We are living in wonderful times. The graduating class of 2000 A.D.*

> *Ever Yours in God,*
> *Blessings on your work,*
> *Hilda*

If there was ever a day that I needed to receive a love letter from Hilda, that was the one. I don't think she consciously knew what was going on in my life. I believe that God spoke to her heart, and she listened, and acted.

I looked again at the letter and saw that it was posted with a St. Francis stamp I had given her. Then I noticed a most lovely fragrance. I held the letter close to my face and I recognized Hilda's delightful rose perfume. It was all of her to all of me. I never received a letter from Hilda before that day, or after.

The last time I saw Hilda, she gave me her final gift. Having moved to Hawaii and been traveling a great deal, I hadn't seen Hilda for over a year. The night before I was to arrive in New York on a tour, I phoned Hilda to let her know I would be coming to her class. "How wonderful, darling!" she responded, "I wish I would have known you were coming earlier—I would have turned the whole class over to you. Please come and speak on anything you like."

When I arrived, I saw that Hilda had set up a chair next to her on the stage. I was treated as an honored person. It was all a little hard for me to take. I didn't feel like an eminent person; I felt like one of Hilda's kids coming home to put my head on mama's shoulder after a long time in a far country. But she wouldn't let me be small. Hilda made a big fuss over me and introduced me as if I were an important sage or teacher. She turned the floor over to me.

When I stood up to speak, all I could think about was how much I appreciated Hilda and all the graces she had shown me over the years. I told about the time I found her letter in my mailbox, about how my life had been transformed from a fearful struggle to a continuous joy, about how Hilda's vision of the God in me had inspired me to create, to heal, and to love. That was my way of bearing witness to all the miraculous blessings I had received through being with Hilda. I didn't know that would be the last time I would see her. And if I had known, that is exactly what I would have said.

When I sat down after speaking, Hilda kissed me and thanked me as if I had done her a big favor just by being there. Again I wondered why she was making such a big fuss about me. "Doesn't she see my frailties, my problems, my hypocrisy?" I puzzled. Then it dawned on me that *she didn't*. I realized that she was seeing me in such a totally different way than I had always seen myself, that one of us had to be wrong. I saw that if one of us had the wrong idea about who I was, it must be me. Then I understood that although there seemed to be many lessons over all the years I was with her, there was really only one: *the vision of perfection*. My soul had enrolled to study with Hilda to discover and believe in my own divinity, and that night was graduation. If I had any doubts about my beauty, my goodness, or my importance as a minister of God in this world, that night those doubts were erased by Hilda's love and her vision of my holiness. No greater gift is possible in this world.

And now, what of Hilda's passing? The week before she moved on to her new life, I had gone to see the movie, *Batteries Not Included*. The film is a delightful story of a group of people who are being evicted from the home they know and love. Each one, in his or her own way, prays for some kind of help. Soon they receive it in the form of some adorable little flying saucers.

There is one marvelous scene in the movie in which the "mama" saucer is teaching her children to fly. Like a mother robin, she takes the children to the highest floor of the apartment house and nudges them off the landing. The first two children quickly learn the art of flying, but the baby is more reluctant. He hangs on to the banister in every possible way, resisting mama's attempts to push him into independent flight. Finally she quits her gentle efforts and gets out a hacksaw. The mother saws off a portion of the railing to which her child is clinging. The board splits off and finally baby has no choice: Fly or fall. He flies.

In a way, I and Hilda's other students have had the last bit of the railing cut away. It is time for us to fly on our own, to graduate from studentship to mastery. No longer can we lean on Hilda's body; now we must take refuge in her essence, which is ours. That spirit was always with us, but all of us suffered the illusion of identifying her essence with her body. Now we are free to learn who Hilda is, and who we really are.

I have no possible way to know how many souls Hilda touched, how many spiritual seekers' lives she changed, how many healings she performed, how many miracles she created. I can't guess how many psychotherapy patients were able to release themselves from long-term therapy, how many marriages she saved, or how many people in despair changed their mind about jumping off a bridge after even a brief talk with her. I know of many, and I am sure there are many more I don't know of.

I do know that my books and workshops, inspired by her presence and her teachings, have touched hundreds of thousands of people. I do know that a doctor in New Jersey, with Hilda's spiritual support, has succeeded in legislating the banning of radioactive mining and radioactive treatment of foods in the state. I do know that there are psychologists, policemen, teachers, parents, musicians, artists, scientists, and ministers who wake up each morning with a new song in their heart. And now they go to work and live with their families with a new, deeper belief in themselves. They shine with the confidence that God is working through them as they open their hearts to love and to serve as Hilda loved and served them. I can think of no greater tribute to Hilda's life on earth and the teachings that she stood for and lived for, than to know that endless miracles are continuing to happen because she believed in us as she believed in God.

*Hilda in meditation*

# Section Six

# *All the Way Home*

# A GENTLE
# TRANSITION

*Death has no power over the spirit.*
*Nothing has power over the spirit.*
*We are spiritual beings, and*
*no matter what seems to be*
*happening in the physical world,*
*who we truly are is always*
*very much alive, whole, and in love.*

*Jeane Cohen*

There is no death. What was never born can never die. That which is truly alive lives eternally. Sometimes it is only when we look upon death face to face that we can see that the grim reaper is nothing more than a wispy shadow.

Before my dear mother Jeane passed on, her death was one of the events that I feared most. Now that it has happened, I have found strength and healing through it.

When, at the depth of her illness, I received a phone call from the hospital telling me that Jeane's insurance had run out and I would have to take her home, I was stunned. It was the day before Christmas and I was lucky to get the first-aid squad to give her a ride to her apartment.

"What am I to do?" I deliberated. I knew that my place was with her. I had no idea how much longer she would be in this world. But whether it was a day or a week or a year, I knew my place was with her.

For a hellish yet liberating week, I watched my mother die. Daily she withered and lost control of her functions and ability to communicate through her body. It was a week during which I learned so much more than any other week, and one I would never want to repeat.

During that week our relationship grew deeper and more powerful than ever. As our physical communication diminished, our spiritual connection became very real. It became clear to me that the body is one of the lesser ways through which real communication occurs.

When my mom finally passed on, I was amazed by the ease and simplicity of the process. Jeane breathed in, she breathed out, and she did not breathe in again. I felt for her pulse and it was absent. This was the moment I had dreaded, and now it seemed so gentle. There was no turning back.

My first impulse was to run for help. I dashed out of my mom's apartment and ran out the door of the building to see if I could catch the visiting nurse, who had left just minutes earlier. She was gone. I stood at the door, looking into the street, wondering if there was something else I should do. A voice within me spoke gently: "Let it be."

I realized this was a perfect opportunity for me to be with my mom in the most precious and intimate way. Here, at the very moment of her transition, I could say goodbye and honor her and our relationship in a way that was real and meaningful for me.

I went back up to her apartment and sat down in the soft white chair next to her bed. I took a deep breath and relaxed as well as I could. Then I began to speak to Jeane in my mind. I told her of my love for her, how deeply I appreciated all she had shared with me, and, most of all, I wished her well. I blessed my mom as I envisioned her setting off on the next stage of her great journey. The adventure we call life, I knew, did not end with the body. Even though I could not see her physically, I knew she was very present.

I lit a candle. It made much of the darkness disappear. Then I turned my mind toward God. With each breath I saw the room filling with a golden light, and I offered love and support to Jeane as she entered her new home. A great peace pervaded the room. There was nothing fearful about this thing we call death.

I opened my eyes and I looked at my mom's body. Already the symptoms of death had begun to set in. Her lips had turned a darker hue. When I touched her cheek, it was cold. How quickly the body crumbled without the spirit to animate it.

I sat back and began to consider who or what it was that I was looking at. As I gazed upon Jeane's lifeless form, I felt a sense of emptiness and loss. Yet as I continued to observe, the sadness turned into a sense of release. "Could this be my mother?" I asked myself. "Is the body I am looking at the one who loved me, who challenged me, the one who was there for me when I was hurting? Did those arms nurture me? Did those lips bless my forehead as I went to sleep as a child? Was that body really my mother?"

The more I looked, the more I thought, and the more I considered, the clearer it became that what I looked upon was not my mother. What my body's eyes beheld was but a form, the vessel through which my mother gave me the love and caring that was so precious to me. Here was the body, but something was absent. That all-important something was the spirit, the life force, the being that was, and continues to be, a wonderful soul known as Jeane Cohen. With that realization came a great freedom. My mother was not the body I had identified her as being; she had simply lived in it. Just because Jeane's body came to an end did not mean that she did. So much for death.

But that is not the end of the story—it never is. For every death, there is a lesson in life.

Jeane has continued to speak to me, in my heart, in my mind, in my dreams, and in conversations through my clairvoyant friend, Carla.

"Your mother says she likes your new home!" Carla conveyed to me. "Wear your galoshes"; "You don't eat right"; and "She's a nice girl— you should stick with her" have been some of the messages which confirmed that my mom is very much with me. (Those were the same comments she made when she inhabited her body.) Life does go on!

Perhaps the most cogent testimony of Jeane's continued loving presence was a gift I received from her. One day when I was speaking to Carla on the telephone, she asked me, "Have you received the present from your mom yet?"

I didn't recall receiving any mail without a postmark. "Not that I know of."

"You will," Carla assured me. "I was in a gift shop in St. Louis. As I passed by a certain item, your mom whispered in my ear that I should get it for you. I have no idea what it is, but I was happy to follow her advice. You should receive it soon."

I was stumped. What could my mom have sent me from the spirit world?

Before she had passed, my mom had a *mezuzah* which she had asked me to post for her. A *mezuzah* is a Jewish religious object, a small box about the size of an index finger. It contains a holy parchment and it is traditionally affixed to the doorpost of a home, serving to bless those entering and leaving the house. Although my mom had repeatedly asked me to put up her *mezuzah*, I had never successfully completed the job. When she passed on, the *mezuzah* was left lying in her kitchen drawer.

You can imagine my surprise and delight, then, when I received a package from Carla. I opened it to find a *mezuzah* similar to my mom's. No one had ever known about my mom's mezuzah but Jeane and me. This, to me, was a clear and loving sign that Jeane was with me wherever I was—and she expected that *mezuzah* to be posted. (Even death cannot keep a Jewish mother off the job!)

As I have shared these experiences with people in my workshops, many have told me that they have gone through similar portals of learning. They have discovered, as I did, that death has no power over the spirit. Nothing has power over the spirit. We are spiritual beings. No matter what seems to be happening in the physical world, who we truly are is always very much alive, whole, and in love.

That was lesson number one of my mom's gentle transition. Lesson number two is: Make sure you put your mom's *mezuzah* up the first time she asks you.

*Alan and Jeane*

# THE FLOWER
# IN THE ROCK

*Our times are miracle times. They are a
call for stronger love, richer compassion,
and deeper joining. The rock is there,
but so is the flower. And we are free
to choose which we will behold.*

## If Old Men Told the Truth

I recently met a retired Air Force colonel who had his own nuclear bomb. "I used to be the commander of an airplane designed for war," he told me. "I believed that the greatest day of my career was when I was given a plane with an atomic bomb in it, along with a flight plan depicting where to drop that bomb on the Russian people.

"I don't think that way any more," he told me. "Through experiencing war, I have learned that there is no glory in it. Wars are perpetuated only because most people don't observe them firsthand. The best way to end a conflict that the government glorifies would be to televise it and show all the people what is actually happening. If people saw the horror that war really is, there would be such a cry for peace that the government would have to get out of the way and let the people have it. It is true that 'If old men told the truth about war, young men would never go.' "

## From Disillusionment to Truth

We are living in an amazing time. It is a time when there is no more room for secrets, closet identities, hidden histories, or private actions. Consider the scandals of the past few decades: The exposure of the agony of the Vietnam conflict. Watergate. The Iran Contra deals. The revelations of the hidden sexual and financial activities of television evangelists, and the subsequent fall of these religious idols. The divulgence of plagiarism in politics. The growing awareness of the incidence of child abuse. The list goes on.

When I first learned of these scandals, I felt shocked, disappointed, and somewhat demoralized. I could not understand how these people whom I had trusted and been taught to respect without question—government leaders, religious teachers, and parents—could live in ways that were exactly opposite the roles and models I believed they were to fulfill. On a broader level, these exposés have rocked our nation's and our world's sense of security. Many of us have reeled in confusion, wondering, "Who can I trust, anyway?"

There is an empowering way to look at the upheavals we have been experiencing—a way that brings us from bitterness to strength. While the changes around us have been immediately painful, they have ultimately been helpful. We have learned that hiding doesn't work, and that holding the hidden up to the light is healing.

We are in the process of coming to greater integrity, more strength of character, and wholeness. As limiting myths fall by the wayside, we are discovering more of the truth of who we really are and the way we want to live in the world. To the follower of fear, disillusionment is an abyss. To the learner of love, when an illusion goes, a shining truth stands in its place.

## The Lifting of the Curtain

We are told that we are living in the time of the Apocalypse. The word "apocalypse" means "the unveiling"—the revealing of that which has been hidden. Seeing in the light what has been in the dark. The word says nothing about fear, punishment, or the wrath of God. It indicates clarity, the presence of wisdom, and the advent of broader vision.

If you have been afraid of the Apocalypse, this is the good news you have been waiting for: The Apocalypse is the lifting of the curtain, the shining of awareness on the fears that have kept us in spiritual bondage. It is the seeing in light that allows us to bless and transform what once held power over us in the dark. The Apocalypse undoes the last vestige of night before the morning.

## Birth Pangs of a Healed World

When planting a garden, the most difficult part is the initial breaking up of hardened earth. This dramatic upheaval prepares and softens the ground so new seeds may be planted. What we are now seeing in the crumbling of institutions around us is the turning over of the ground of consciousness, the breaking up of clods of fear. The old forms of government, economics, and religion are not big or strong enough to hold the power of what is to come. They are the old wineskins into which new wine cannot be poured, lest they break. And that is wonderful, for what is to come bears far more power, integrity, and reality than what has been.

A world based on hiding is bound to be dissolved when the light comes. There is the appearance of great chaos and mass confusion. Immense change comes quickly; sometimes we feel unprepared. We are being moved into new and awesome roles in the cosmos. We wonder what is happening, and why?

These changes are the birth pangs of a new way of being on the planet. Many are hearing the call, and many are dulled to it. Those of us who hear are stepping forward to claim our vision. Those who do not hear now will one day awaken. Each of us must be true to our own heart's calling. There are no more outer references. The outer world is important only as a manifestation of our inner vision. We see truly only with our heart.

## The Poem of God

One morning as Karren and I were hiking past a waterfall, she exclaimed, "Look!"

I looked—and what I saw was wondrous indeed! Out of a nearly sheer rock wall there grew a flower. I traced the stem to find the soil in which this little poem of God was rooted. I could not see any. When I touched the flower, I found it was strong and vibrantly healthy. Somehow this graceful little creature had implanted itself in a rock and found a way to grow.

I began to think about how it is possible for a thing of beauty to grow out of a rocky situation. This did not seem like a likely place for a blossom to unfold, but thank God the flower seed knew better! It chose to find a home where safety did not seem assured. Of all the flowers in this lush valley, this one stood out to me as one of special preciousness: It was a statement that courage is seeded by choice, not circumstance.

The flower in the rock gave me inspiration to bless the changes through which we are courageously moving. If our times seem painful, it is not because the darkness is overtaking us. It is because the light is coming closer, and we still have fear. The best way to move through fear is to embrace it as a messenger with a gift. Let us be gracious and open to receive the gift so we may move on quickly to greater joy and richer life.

Our times are miraculous times. They are a call for stronger love, richer compassion, and deeper joining. The rock is there, but so is the flower. And we are free to choose which we will behold.

# THIS IS
# YOUR DREAM

*It's time for you to quit being an
extra in other people's movies,
and start being the star of your own.*

In a dream, I was presenting a workshop in which some people began to criticize the way I was teaching. At first I sloughed off the disapproval, but when more people attacked me, I became upset. "What is going on here?" I wondered. "Why are these people against me?"

One who had been attacking me approached me, put his arm around my shoulder and whispered in my ear, "Why are you upset? This is *your* dream...You can have it any way you want."

*This is your dream.* Your movie. It's your life, unfolding just as you create it. There was a popular song, *"Any way you want it—that's the way it's gonna be."* I wonder if the Dave Clark Five realized they were teaching a great truth. Moment by moment we write the script of our own story. The characters who people our dream are simply the manifestations of our own ideas, cast onto the screen of the world by the projector of our mind. And we learn from them all.

What kind of dream would you like to play in? *A Course in Miracles* tells us that we have the power to create a happy dream. Dreams, like movies, are subject to the creativity of the executive producer. You have executive power over your production. What kind of movies have you produced? Dramas? Soap operas? Romantic comedies? Biblical epics? Adventures? Science fiction? Cult films? Boring documentaries? All of the above? No matter what kind of movie you have been producing, or how meager the roles you have accepted, you can recreate the story to express the true desires of your heart. *You can quit being an extra in other people's movies and become the star of your own.*

Charley and Lori Thweatt sing a dynamic song:

> *Take your power back, that you've been given*
> *Get it back, like you had it before*
> *Take your power back, that you've been given*
> *Get it back, and you'll have even more.*[12]

We must take our power back. We have given our power away to people, beliefs, and objects outside ourself, and we need to reclaim it. If you succeed at anything, it is because you have chosen to do so, and if you fail, it is also your choice. At any time, no matter what choices you have made in the past, you can—and will—choose again. You are always free to choose a different future.

## Sin Boldly

T.S. Elliot said, *"Only those who dare to go too far can possibly find out how far one can go."* Dare to go too far. You are much bigger than you thought you were, and you can accomplish much more than you thought. Laugh at the past. It was a dream. If it was a bad dream, thank God that you have awakened. If it was a good dream, dare God and yourself to make it even more spectacular.

God loves outrageous people. The Bible clearly demonstrates that the Creator enjoys Her most feisty children: Quite a few of the saints, sages, and prophets were pretty flamboyant characters—prostitutes, murderers, thieves, and slinky used camel salesmen. It was rare that God chose a boring person to bring The Message to the world; after all, who would listen to a deadbeat? Just consider: If you were the Lord and you needed a messenger, would you hire a nerd? Of course not. You would choose some vibrant personality with a history of successful sin, and blow the expectations of the masses by transforming him or her into an open-hearted saint. Then you would show this clever person how to re-apply the skills they gained on the streets and put them on your payroll as a teacher and healer. Not a bad recruitment plan for world healing.

A friend of mine has a bumper sticker on her washing machine advising, *"Sin boldly."* To me this is not a temptation to deny God; it is an invitation to act with a whole and vibrant heart, to make our life a dynamic testament to realizing our vision. We learn more quickly and deeply by following our own inner voice than by attempting to please other people or live in belief systems that do not correspond with our own being.

The Holy Spirit respects those who engage in whatever they're doing with an enthusiastic heart, even if it does not look right to the world. God is neither intimidated by nor angry with sinners; like manure, sin is a great fertilizer for some wonderfully nourishing crops. An accomplished sinner is good raw material for sainthood. There have been very few saints who have been holy from childhood. Most saints are made, not born. The great Paramahansa Yogananda declared, "A saint is a sinner who never gave up."

Don't give up. By nature, we're not sinners, but we have thought we are. Every limitation we have ever felt has been self-imposed. God has never stopped anyone from being great—only fear has. And in the long run, we can see how the fears that held us back ultimately created the pressure that catapulted us forward to our highest destiny. When we get fed up with feeling limited, we pop out of our shell of littleness and claim who we really are.

It's a new movie. We're waking up together. Actually, the reel is more like a videotape than a film: At any given moment we can tape over it and make a new picture. We are always free to choose a different future. Let us empower one another to create the dream, the movie, the vision that is true to our self. As we follow our heart, we inspire and help others to do the same. In God's movie, *everyone* has a leading role. God's is the only dream in which *everyone* wins.

We are not alone, and we don't need luck. We just need to remember who we are. Remember: This is your dream. You might as well have it be the one you want.

# FROM HELL
# TO HEAVEN

*Love is the great healing power of life.*
*To be in love is to be truly empowered.*
*To extend love is to truly empower.*
*There is nothing that shared love cannot heal.*

I saw a magazine ad describing the Corporate Angel Network (CAN), a volunteer organization which provides free air transportation for cancer patients who need to get treatment in cities far from their home. The advertisement noted that over 325 corporations have offered cancer patients space on their private jets.

I am deeply touched and inspired by this project. To me, CAN represents how we are all going to make it. If we are to be saved from our personal and planetary predicament—and we are—it will be through one another.

On the *Merv Griffin Show*, Merv asked the channeled entity Ramtha, "Will there be a second coming?"

Ramtha leaned onto Merv's desk, purposefully caught his eyes, and answered, "Yes—and it will come through you."

Ramtha did not mean that Merv alone is the savior. No one alone is the savior. What we call the New Age, the Millennium, or the Golden Era, is founded on the awakening of the Christ consciousness in *everyone*, the acceptance and celebration of the light within *all of us*.

### The Potential of Willingness

I met a woman who was about to set out on the Great Peace March. 1,500 people dedicated themselves to walk across the country for nine months as a statement of their commitment to world peace, including nuclear disarmament. The marchers set out from Los Angeles, toughed it out over the Rockies, trekked across the continent, and completed their grand statement with a rally in Washington, D.C.

The woman told me that at first her husband wasn't pleased with the idea of her going for nine months, but ultimately he supported her. Like Mrs. Gandhi and Mrs. King supported their spouses. The Great March.

I feel a deep sense of awe as I consider the power that an act such as the Great Peace March releases into the universe. *A Course in Miracles* explains that whenever we offer a miracle of love, it ripples out, touching many, many persons in ways that we are not aware of. This is the potential of our willingness to empower one another by standing for what we believe in.

## What Do We Live For?

When I met the Native American teacher Sun Bear, he suggested a thoughtful way to make the world lighter: Put a coin in someone's parking meter that is going overtime. I love that idea, as it symbolizes the kind of way we can bring more joy into our lives; ways that seem small, but are actually very grand. As T. S. Elliot put it, "What do we live for, if not to make life easier for one another?"

I am discovering the preciousness of every moment of my life. More and more I am finding the blessing in every interaction and relationship. Take close encounters of the toll booth kind, for example. There is a game that I love to play, called "Juice the Toll Collector." Sometimes toll collectors can be a little down; the job can get to be mechanical, cold, and impersonal. My game is to make contact with the heart of the person standing inside the booth.

As the toll collector hands me my change, I'll tell them something encouraging, like "Thanks for working on New Year's Day today," or "I appreciate you doing a good job," or I'll make a little joke if I can. I have found that it really works! I enjoy seeing the collector's face light up as they feel acknowledged and appreciated. Sometimes I look in my rear view mirror as I drive away, and I can see them leaning out of the booth, waving.

I like to feel that I have made the most of my 15 seconds with that person, and that both of our lives are richer because of it. I do it as much for myself as for them. I need to feel connected with them, and I am glad to be able to do something that helps me feel that joining.

A woman I know made friends with a particular toll collector when she took the same route to pick up her children from school each day. The tollman and the family became close friends. On a recent birthday of one of the children, the family was touched to receive a loving present in the mail from their friend in the toll booth. What a marvelous example of how we can make the routine activities of our days alive with the heartful spirit in which we want to live!

## Through the Heart

The difference between a saint and a sourpuss is that the sourpuss sees his daily interactions as a nuisance, while the saint finds a continuous stream of opportunities to celebrate. One finds intruders, the other angels. At any given moment we have the power to choose what we will be and what we will see. Each of us has the capacity to find holiness or attack in all about us.

The way out of pain is through the heart. We need to feel the preciousness of our own being and that of those we touch. We need each other. Not one of us can do it all by ourself or make it to God alone. We are blessed by our interdependence. Each of us has a gift for the rest of us. Will we deny our sisters' and brothers' blessings because of our judgments or preconceived notions of how they, or life, should be? While our souls are very wise, our reasoning minds do not see very far down the road. But there is One who sees with a great perspective, and this One brings us to delight through the gifts we share with one another.

Love is the great healing power of life. To be in love is to be truly empowered. To extend love is to truly empower. There is nothing that shared love cannot heal or overcome. Herein lies our safety, comfort, and destiny.

### From Hell to Heaven

There is a story about a man who passed from this world, and found himself on a tour of the higher realms. The man's guide opened a door and showed him a room in which a group of people had a large and delicious banquet spread before them. To the man's astonishment, he saw that all of these people were starving. The spoons they were trying to eat with were longer than their arms, and they could not get the food into their mouths.

"This," explained the guide, "is hell."

"That's terrible!" remarked the visitor. "Please show me heaven."

The guide took him to another room. There he saw exactly the same banquet— except that the faces in this room were smiling and the tummies were full. The visitor looked more carefully to see why these people were happy. Then he found it: Here the people had learned to feed one another.

# THE POWER
# OF JOINING

*While our current dilemma has posed the*
*gravest danger to our planet in history,*
*it has also offered us the greatest opportunity:*
*Join or die. Communicate or disappear.*
*Become one or lose it all. It's a*
*planetary initiation. And it's a gift.*

McDonald's is coming to Moscow. It's official. This fall, the first Russian hamburger palace will be built in the capital city of the Soviet Union. Typically Russian, it will be huge—a whopping 620 seater. The featured product? A *Bolshoi Mac*. *Bolshoi*, meaning big. Six more fast-food eateries under the golden arches will follow there within the next few years. No McKidding.

Now I *know* there will not be a war. The United States would not drop nuclear missiles on its own interests. We would not bomb ourselves. The Hindus may have been correct after all. Cows may indeed be sacred—they may save the world!

On my last visit to Moscow I was told that Pizza Hut and hotel mogul Donald Trump are both close to beginning businesses behind the formerly iron curtain. That curtain is now being raised. I also learned that, for the first time, Soviet citizens are able to obtain mortgages to buy their own homes.

I think we have to hand it to business. In the old days we believed that war could be averted by aggressively overpowering smaller people and nations. Later we attempted to stop war by marching against it. Now we are seeing firsthand that peace is coming through *joining*. By allowing part of us to become part of them. By perceiving our interests to be the same, rather than separate.

Several years ago *New Frontier Magazine* featured an article suggesting that the surest way to avoid a war between the Americans and the Soviets would be to have each country exchange citizens. The United States would invite thousands of Soviets to live with our families, work, and play among us. Likewise, we would send our people to share the Soviets' lifestyle. The purpose behind the exchange is simple: We would never dispatch bombs to kill our own people, and neither would the Soviets. Ultimately, real healing will occur when we discover that we are all alike anyway. The Soviets are our own people, and we are theirs.

In the Chinese language, the written character for the word "crisis" is a combination of the characters for "danger" and "opportunity." In every apparent danger, there is a rich opportunity. The greater the danger, the deeper the opportunity for transformation and healing.

While our nuclear dilemma has, to be sure, posed the greatest danger to our planet in its history, it has also offered the greatest opportunity: join or die. Communicate or disappear. Become one or lose it all. It's a planetary initiation. And it's a gift.

While some of us have cursed technology, computers, and business as evils that will destroy the world, the Holy Spirit has a use for these activities. Ultimately, they will be used in the service of healing our planet. The same technology that created nuclear warheads has given us the ability to travel to the other side of the globe in just a few hours; to see and hear one another instantaneously; to learn, teach, and store valuable information that has assisted us in shifting our attention from survival to communication and development. Learning about each other is always good, for seeing each other clearly ultimately brings us to the realization that we are all one. The way that we keep enemies is by choosing not to look at them. As we have seen more and more of the Russians, and they of us, we have learned that they are not who we were taught they were, and neither are we.

McDonald's in Moscow. Pizza Hut in Leningrad. The Dodgers versus the Comrades in the '99 World Series. Perhaps we have been somewhat audacious in calling our national series the World Series. Up until now we haven't invited the rest of the world to play. But now it's a different game. What we thought was "out there" is really *in here*. We have met the enemy, and it is not a person or a nation, but fear. And the only real antidote to fear is love. As we express love through business, we recognize that our only real business is love.

# THE TIME
# OF LIGHT

*Our job is not to convert others, but to
transform ourself. As each of us finds
peace in our own heart, we begin to
radiate a light that warms and heals
everyone we contact. This is the
way of the planetary healer.*

As I consider the holiday season, I am touched by the fact that it is the one time of the year when two of the world's major religions are joined in the celebration of light on the planet. The birth of the Christ represents the awakening of the light within our hearts. Hanukkah is the festival of light, commemorating the miracle of a small vat of holy oil burning for an unexpected eight days during a time of darkness for the Jewish people.

I find it fascinating that both holidays come around the winter solstice, when the days start to lengthen after reaching their shortest point. This is the time of year when the darkness has reached it maximum, and now the night must give way to the morning.

It is said that man's extremity is God's opportunity, that the lowest ebb is the turn of the tide. When the darkness is deepest, we have our greatest opportunity for a miracle. It is when we seem to be up against a wall that Spirit finds Its most powerful opening to do for us what we cannot do for ourselves.

## Angels About and Within

During the holiday—holy day—season, we enjoy the most poignant public acknowledgement of angels. Years ago my spiritual teacher Hilda told me that angels are the most present with us on the planet around this time, as we open the door to their reality and draw them into our midst with song, celebration, and the spirit of giving.

Considering that everything we see in the outer world is the manifestation of an inner process, there is a great symbolism to the angelic presence during this season. We have come to the point on our planet where we must own and accept responsibility for our own angelic nature. For thousands of years, through religion and song, we have honored and worshipped the angels that abide around us. We see them in visions, paint them in masterful works of art, and laud their divinity in classical choruses. We recognize them by their magnificent wings, we honor their heavenly halos, and we humbly bow in the presence of their cherubic countenance.

But what about the angels with hands and feet, the cherubs who wear blue jeans and workshirts, and the industrious spirits who carry briefcases on the subway?

What about the furry little seraphs with four legs who prance up to us and kiss us excitedly when we come home from a hard day's work? Or the winged singers who sit on their balconies of branches and call us to awaken to a new day? These tuneful messengers bring us bright color and a fresh song to brighten and warm a cold winter's day.

And what about the angels of noble intention who have stepped into public office, courageously entering the battlefield of politics, attempting to bring about real peace in the world?

What about those angels who cut us off on the highway, or challenge us with harsh words or an irritating presence? Do they not urge us to delve deeper into ourself to find a peace that is not vulnerable to worldly changes? And then there are the guardians who teach through painful experiences, requiring us to find a godly strength within our soul, a power that we would not have mobilized unless it were drawn forth through trial.

And then what about every person we encounter? Surely they carry the spark of the divine. They offer us opportunities to find beauty and join with them in spirit. God comes to us in the elevator, through the smile of the man who hands us the change for our newspaper, and through the receptionist whose voice we hear on the other end of the telephone.

Hilda told us of a job she had during World War II where she served as a telephone receptionist in a factory. She made it her meditation to page employees with the sweetest intonation she could express. "Mr. Jones, you have a telephone call. Please pick up the nearest telephone. Thank you." She made her announcements over the company loudspeaker in the most songlike voice possible. She recalled that at the end of each day many of the people she paged thanked her for the kind and loving way in which she called their names. Truly she brought an angelic quality to what could have been an otherwise mundane job.

## From Worship to Worthship

We must acknowledge ourselves as angels, too. Could it be that so many in the outer world are angelic, but we retain the only dark spot in a universe of light? It is not so. Let us recognize and celebrate the angels that we are, the beings of holy light that we were born to express. This is our true purpose and gift to the world. Let us stand in full acknowledgement of the holy, innocent beings that we are, and the grand goal for which we have come to earth: to shine the light of love upon all that we see and touch.

I know that the celestial angels take deep delight when we celebrate our equality with them. They do not seek to be worshipped, nor do they want to have to keep saving us from troubles we create when we forget who we are. I am certain that they would rather play with us than have to keep praying for us. I know that the God who created us all, visible and invisible, would agree. Spirit has plenty of unseen cherubs to staff the etheric realms. Love needs the rest of us to draw blessings into the physical world.

Let's experiment with how many miracles we can create by knowing and acting as if God is working through us. We must never underestimate the power of a kind act. Mahatma Gandhi said that the pure loving kindness of one gentle soul can nullify the hatred of millions. Surely his life was a demonstration of this truth. Now we are called to access the fullness of our own potential.

## The Power of Agreement

The way to accomplish healing is to be aware of similarities, not differences. On my recent visit to the Soviet Union, I discovered that the most powerful form of diplomacy is to focus on how we are alike. During our interactions with the Soviets, I noticed that when we discussed experiences of a common nature—our families, jobs, and aspirations for peace—there was a great feeling of harmony and excitement in the room. Somehow we were lifted out of our divergent histories and united in our dream of a common destiny. When the conversation delved into political or moral discussions, however, participants began to take sides, polarity occurred, and we clearly lost the sense of joining for a common purpose. The feeling in the room would go "thud."

There was one person in our group who was consistently a messenger of peace. When Mira, age six months, came into the room, everyone lit up. The political debates stopped, and for a precious moment everyone looked at the baby and smiled. There was an immediate recognition of the light that she brought with her, and the power of her innocence melted any vestiges of political tension. Wherever we went, the Russian people loved to look at Mira, and they put aside their chores to play with her. The waitresses in the dining room, although sometimes harsh and gruff in their service, put down their trays and playfully argued over who would get to hold the child while we dined. The illusion of barriers melted, and there we were—just people enjoying being together. I wondered how we could have ever seen each other as enemies.

### *Just for Today*

We can do most for planetary healing by acknowledging the unity of all religions and peoples. While religion was intended to be a way to bring people together, it has more often been used to separate hearts that are literally dying to love one another. More wars have been fought in the name of God than for any other reason. I do not believe that God was behind any of them. God is on everyone's side, and no one's. God is another name for uniting and healing hearts that have been divided by fear.

During World War I the French and German armies called a truce on Christmas. Both armies laid down their guns and had dinner together in a local tavern. They shared food, drink, and song in little towns near the battlefield. The next day they went back to shooting each other. But for one day, one time of light, the darkness was consciously put aside by people who were bigger than their difference. Together, they sat and loved one another as brothers. Their fears fell by the wayside, and their oneness became their reality.

I propose a truce that continues one day at a time. It may be hard for us to imagine calling a permanent truce, but what if we decided not to fight—just for today? And then, when tomorrow comes, what if we again decide not to fight—just for that day? And the next day we can decide not to fight again—just for that day. Before long, we might find that peace is a reality because we were willing to choose it—just for today.

You do not have to make peace for the whole world. That project may seem overwhelming—and it is. Our job is not to convert others, but to transform ourself. As each of us finds peace in our own heart, we begin to radiate a light that warms and heals everyone we contact, by virtue of the peace they feel in our presence. This is the way of the planetary healer. You and I are among the chosen. The chosen are those who choose themselves to be peaceful.

# THE POINT
# OF BIRTH

*It is only a matter of time until what now seems empty will come to bloom. A rosebush in winter appears barren and stark only because we see, with our inner eye, the full beauty of the blossoming flower as it was—and shall be.*

## The Mountaintop Vision

I remember how I felt after my first spiritual retreat. I was high as a kite. I just wanted to be in love, keep my heart open, and celebrate with the whole world. During one powerful weekend, my life shifted 180 degrees for the better. I felt as if the old fearful me had died, and the radiantly beautiful me emerged in its place. I was in love with life, and life was in love with me. It was a thrilling divine romance.

Then, to my surprise, I found the experience beginning to fade. Within a few weeks I saw myself returning to many of my old patterns. Like stubborn weeds, my old habits began to take root again. I began to feel depressed. "What has happened to that great high?" I wondered.

What happened was that the vision was giving way to the practice. I had seen the view from the mountaintop, and so I knew the reality and value of where I was headed. There was no going back to being satisfied with living in fear and hiding. My job now was to set out on the adventure of climbing the mountain of my consciousness, and become the master of the mountain rather than a brief tourist.

You, too, have probably had a breakthrough, or "peak" experience—one in which you felt as if you reached a new plateau of understanding, or entered a deeper and more satisfying awareness. This feeling may have lasted a few seconds, hours, or days. You felt on top of the world, as if you were freed from a long struggle. Then, sooner or later you found yourself heading (maybe even rolling) down the mountain of enlightenment toward your former, less satisfying way of being. At such a moment you may have felt disappointed or discouraged, wondering if what had happened was real, and if you would ever enjoy that wonderful feeling again.

## The Divine Carrot

Do not despair. There is a purpose and a promise in your experience. Let us step back in time for a moment to illustrate:

Do you remember the old *Little Rascals* films? In those delightful adventures, the kids got a goat to pull a cart for them. They trained the goat by hanging a carrot on a stick in front of the animal. The carrot was hung just close enough so the goat could get an occasional nibble, but then, when he had gotten a bite, the kids would move the carrot just far enough ahead of him so he would have to keep reaching out and pulling the cart to get some more.

An experience of sudden awakening is like a divine carrot: We have a life-changing taste of a new joy or openness, and that becomes the prime motivating force in our life. We feel that there is nothing more important than finding that contentment again. The key to this noble goal is that now we must bring our life into harmony. If we want to make peace our own, we must *let go of our old way of thinking and acting, and move ahead to live in the kind of world we now value.* That movement means aligning our thoughts with the principles of healing and keeping our heart open to love.

## The Point of Birth

In the Bible we are asked an intriguing question: *"Shall God bring us to the point of birth, and not deliver?"* Put another way, "Would God start a project that He did not plan to complete?" Or, "Would Spirit give us a vision that the God in us could not bring to life?" I find the Bible's question to be a very exciting promise. The promise, to me, means this: If we have an experience of a new consciousness—even a fleeting moment of a new possibility for our life—*it is only a matter of time until we will live in that feeling as a continuous reality.* The experience is a taste—a seed—of a life to come.

If you have had a sudden awakening and are having difficulty maintaining or integrating it into your life as you are now living it, do not turn back or give up. It is quite normal on the spiritual path to find a treasured experience beginning to fade. (Trying to hold onto it makes it slip away even more rapidly!) You can rejoice, however, for this is not the end of the story. The experience is not a tease—it is a preview of coming attractions. One day, after learning to bring all of your daily experiences to the altar of the heart, you will live in that joyous consciousness without interruption.

## Problems are Prayers

If you have a burning question or difficult problem with which you need help, bless it. Consider your problem, pain, or frustration as a prayer. Place it on the altar of God's compassion and give thanks for it. See your discomfort not as a punishment, but as your heart's call for greater understanding. Spirit will show you the answer—but you need to have a question first. Sometimes our dilemma is not that we cannot find answers, but that we do not know what the question is. You have to know what you are truly asking before you can hear the answer. If your question is burning, you are very close to the answer. Questions are our door-knockers at the gate of Heaven. Be assured that Someone is home, and He will answer.

Our challenges are not curses; they are the flames which stir our deepest, often unknown needs to the surface. Your soul's desire for healing is calling for your attention. Healing cannot be accomplished without your participation; otherwise you would never attain the mastership which you came here to learn. An intrinsic step on the spiritual path is to make the hidden visible so you can see how to step out of fear and choose love instead. Your problems are here not to keep you from God, but to bring you closer to Him. Only in the light of greater awareness can you see your answer.

Our job is to keep asking for truth, and to be willing to hear the answer. We must delve into our hearts' true desires; God's angels will meet us at the gate. We don't have to figure it all out—just bless whatever is happening, and ask to receive its gift. Our healing is guaranteed.

The path to enlightenment is like a divine scavenger hunt—every question or problem that we come upon contains the answer in hidden form, as well as directions to the next clue. Seen in this way, life is not a problem to be solved, but a game to be played. God wouldn't give us a question unless He also had an answer in store. It's a package deal.

### Blessing the Seeds

A friend told me that she felt empty because she didn't love Mother Mary as much as she wanted to. I told her, "Your wanting to love Mary *is* loving Mary. Your feeling empty because you don't love her more shows how much you actually *do* love her. If you yearn for her, she is in your heart. The love you feel is your prayer for more of the same feeling. Whatever we love and think about, we are sure to receive more of."

It is only a matter of time until what now seems empty will come to bloom. A rosebush in winter appears barren and stark only because we see, with our inner eye, the full beauty of the blossoming flower as it was—and shall be.

God would not give someone an inspiration for a great work of art, or any project, unless He was prepared to help that person carry it through. I have seen seemingly insurmountable obstacles overcome because someone held to the faith that God would finish a job that Spirit commissioned.

This principle applies to the disciplines, as well. In the practice of yoga, for example, if I can do a new posture for even one second, I feel that I have mastered it. I know that it is only a matter of time and practice until it becomes natural and easy for me. The "imp" has been taken out of the "impossible."

### Let Your Joy Grow

Joy unfolds within us like a divine seedling. When a seed first sprouts, it must be given special attention, nourishment, and protection. When a farmer plants a tree in a field, he surrounds it with a fence so the cows will not trample it. Later, when the tiny plant has grown into a tree, the fence may be removed. Eventually, the tree becomes so grand and mighty that the cows which once threatened it may rest in its shade, rub up against the trunk, and receive comfort and protection from the tree. So, at first, we must devote our attention, heart, and vision to nurture the joy spirit in our life. We must not allow thoughts of fear, limitation, or the illusions of the world to darken the light that glows within us. If we truly hold our vision to live in joy and make happiness our priority rather than pain, our love will grow into a mighty tree, and then a forest which will change the world that once seemed to threaten it. This is how we will lift our planet into the light in which we were born to live.

The barren branches, the old thoughts of "I can't," eventually fall away and become fertilizer for the new growth we desire. The days of fear are numbered. Ram Dass describes our old, limited selves as being like the cowboys in the old western movies. The gunslingers get shot, and we know they're as good as dead, but they have to roll around and kick and holler a bit before it's all over. So it is with old habits. Once we taste the nectar of a new life, the old habits are already on their way out. It is as if an iron door closes behind us, and we couldn't really go back, even if we wanted to. And that is wonderful, because we wouldn't really want to go back anyway. The only real safety lies in moving ahead, and trusting the voice of joy that speaks within our heart.

### *Coming Attractions*

The next time you are blessed with a Divine Carrot—a flash of new insight or awareness—even if it lasts for a brief second, celebrate it! Praise it! Be grateful for it! It means that you are at the point of birth, ready to deliver a new you to the world. God is giving you a preview of a coming attraction. Spirit is showing you who you will be when you get done being who you now think you are. In truth, God is showing you who you already are. It is only a matter of time and consciousness until your vision of your perfection matches God's. He is prepared to wait, in patience and love, until you see yourself in the same Perfect Light that He sees you. It's a marvelous coming attraction—Don't miss the feature!

# Endnotes

1. Michael Stillwater, "Blues Into Gold," from the album *One Light*, Inner Harmony Music, P.O. Box 450, Kula, HI 96790.

2. Matthew Fox, *Original Blessing*, Bear & Company, P.O. Drawer 2860, Santa Fe, NM 87504, 1983.

3. Barry Vissell and Joyce Vissell, *Risk to be Healed*, Ramira Publishing, P.O. Box 1707, Aptos, CA 95001, 1989.

4. Brother Theophane, *Tales of a Magic Monastery*, The Crossroad Publishing Company, 370 Lexington Avenue, NY, NY 10022, 1981.

5. *A Course in Miracles*, Foundation for Inner Peace, P.O. Box 635, Tiburon, CA 94920.

6. Richard Bach, *Illusions: The Adventures of a Reluctant Messiah*, Delacorte Press, New York, 1977.

7. Jerry Jampolsky, *Love Is Letting Go of Fear*, Bantam, 1987.

8. Barry Neil Kaufman and Suzi Lite Kaufman, *Sonrise*, Harper & Row, 1976. The Kaufman's work and teachings are offered by the Option Process Institute and Fellowship, R.D. #1, Sheffield, MA 01257.

9. Ken Blanchard, author of *The One-Minute Manager*, Berkley Publishing Group, 200 Madison Avenue, New York, NY 10016, 1981.

10. Story adapted from Dr. Nelson Decker, *The Great Mystery in the Sky*, Benu, Inc., P.O. Box 6400, San Rafael, CA 94903.

11. Richard Bach, *Jonathan Livingston Seagull*, Avon, 1970.

12. Charley and Lori Thweatt, "Take Your Power Back," from the album *I Offer You My Heart*, Angelight Music, P.O. Box 1444, Santa Cruz, CA 95061-1444, 1988.

The following is a listing of the publications in which the chapters in this book have appeared as articles.

Joy is My Compass—*New Frontier*, September 1987
What They Serve in Heaven—*New Realities*, May/June 1987
A Dream Come True—*New Frontier*, June 1987
I Already Did That—*New Frontier*, December 1987
Near-Life Experiences—*New Frontier*, January 1989
How Angels Fly—*New Frontier*, May 1987
The Gift I Bring You—*Unity*, June 1988
Home for the Holidays—*New Frontier*, November 1987
From Mystery to Mastery—*New Frontier*, March 1987
The Intentional Traveler—*New Frontier*, March 1989
Let It All Be Good—*New Frontier*, November 1988
Nude Frontiers—*New Frontier*, July 1989
I Met the Christ Today—*New Frontier*, June 1988
Where Love Wills—*New Frontier*, December 1988
X-Ray Vision—*American Holistic Medical Association Newsletter*, February 1989
Where Credit is Due—*New Frontier*, July 1987
Room at the Top—*New Frontier*, June 1989
One of Our Boys Made It—not previously published
The City of Refuge—*New Frontier*, April 1987
The Present—*New Frontier*, May 1988
The Counselor—*New Frontier*, May 1989
Born to Love—*New Frontier*, February 1989
True Valentines—*New Frontier*, February 1988
Major League Lovers—*Vision*, June 1989
Real Vision—*New Frontier*, September 1989
The Garden—*Holistic Living*, March/April 1984
The Heaven Game—*New Frontier*, September 1986
Desolation to Development—*New Frontier*, April 1987
Igor's Choice—*New Frontier*, October 1987
Tribute to a Great Soul—*New Frontier*, March 1988
A Gentle Transition—*New Frontier*, September 1988
The Flower in the Rock—*New Frontier*, October 1988
This is Your Dream—*New Frontier*, January 1988
From Hell to Heaven—*New Frontier*, April 1986
The Power of Joining—*New Frontier*, July 1988
The Time of Light—*New Frontier*, December 1986
The Point of Birth—not previously published

# NOTES

# NOTES

# NOTES

# NOTES

# NOTES

# ABOUT THE AUTHOR

**Alan Cohen** is the author of ten popular inspirational books, including the classics *The Dragon Doesn't Live Here Anymore* and *I Had It All the Time*. *The Celestine Prophecy* author James Redfield calls Alan "the most eloquent spokesman of the heart." Alan's column "From the Heart" appears in many New Thought newspapers and magazines internationally, and he is a contributing writer for the best-selling *Chicken Soup for the Soul* series.

Alan resides in Maui, Hawaii, where he conducts seminars on spiritual awakening and visionary living. *The Mastery Training* is a highly focused small group intensive for individuals seeking to bring greater authenticity, love, and integrity to their chosen goals. *Celebrating Paradise* invites participants to reclaim their inner riches in a spirit of greater joy and aliveness. Alan also keynotes and presents workshops at many conferences and expos throughout the United States and abroad.

For a free catalog of Alan Cohen's books and audiocassettes, more information on his Hawaii seminars, and a listing of his upcoming seminars in your area, call (800) 462-3013, or write to Alan in c/o the Publicity Director at Hay House, Inc., P.O. Box 5100, Carlsbad, CA 92018-5100.

To write to Alan Cohen directly or receive more detailed information about his programs, write to The Mastery Foundation, 430 Kukuna Road, Haiku, Hawaii 96708, or call (808) 572-0001.

We hope you enjoyed this Hay House book.
If you would like to receive a free catalog featuring
additional Hay House books and products, or if you would
like information about the Hay Foundation,
please write or call:

Hay House, Inc.
P.O. Box 5100
Carlsbad, CA 92018-5100

**(800) 654-5126**
**(800) 650-5115 (fax)**

**Visit the Hay House Web Site at**
**http://www.hayhouse.com**